Go Programming Cookbook

Over 75+ recipes to program microservices, networking, database and APIs using Golang

Ian Taylor

Copyright © 2024 by GitforGits

All rights reserved. This book is protected under copyright laws and no part of it may be reproduced or transmitted in any form or by any means, electronic or mechanical, including photocopying, recording, or by any information storage and retrieval system, without the prior written permission of the publisher. Any unauthorized reproduction, distribution, or transmission of this work may result in civil and criminal penalties and will be dealt with in the respective jurisdiction at anywhere in India, in accordance with the applicable copyright laws.

Published by: GitforGits
Publisher: Sonal Dhandre
www.gitforgits.com
support@gitforgits.com

Printed in India

First Printing: February 2024

ISBN: 9788119177370

Cover Design by: Kitten Publishing

For permission to use material from this book, please contact GitforGits at support@gitforgits.com.

Prologue

With a single goal in mind, I set out to write the "Go Programming Cookbook"—a resource that would revolutionize the way Go is used by developers of all skill levels. My love for Go programming and my desire to help other programmers find elegant and efficient solutions to common problems inspired me to write this book. If you're lost in the wide ocean of Go programming, this is more than simply a cookbook—it's a guiding light.

My intention all along was to make the otherwise complex world of Go programming easier to understand. The ever-expanding ecosystem, Go's exceptional concurrency support, and the language's innate simplicity have long captivated me. On the other hand, I was cognizant of the difficulties that programmers encounter on a regular basis, such as dealing with dependencies, protecting online applications, and dealing with concurrency issues. My hope is that anyone can overcome these obstacles and become an expert Go programmer with the help of this book.

Starting with the most basic ideas and working your way up to more complex ones, the "Go Programming Cookbook" is structured to systematically increase your knowledge. So that you can use goroutines and channels like an expert, I break down the language's fundamental ideas, show you how to organize your code efficiently, and walk you through Go's concurrency model. An essential part of contemporary programming, networking is broken down to make sure you can build clients and servers, handle protocols with finesse, and secure connections with TLS/SSL.

Any application relies on data durability and manipulation. As a result, I dive into the topic of SQL and NoSQL database integration, highlighting real-world examples to help you simplify your data interactions. In order to help you become a better coder, we've included chapters on dependency management, testing, and error handling. On top of that, optimizing performance is a common thread; it will show you how to profile, manage memory, and benchmark your programs so that they run faster and more efficiently.

The book stands out due of its applicability. The recipes are practical answers to real-world issues, derived from extensive programming knowledge, rather than idle speculation. With their project-specific design, they let you improve and debug your Go scripts for a wide range of uses. In addition to fixing issues right away, following these recipes will teach you excellent practices that will make your code better overall.

I hope that by sharing my knowledge and love of Go with you in this book, I will inspire a similar devotion in you. Discovering, learning, and, at last, mastering, are all parts of the journey. When you finish, you won't just be able to program in Go; you'll know how to fully utilize Go's capabilities, and you'll be confident enough to take on difficult programming problems.

Content

CONTENT	IV
PREFACE	XIV
ACKNOWLEDGEMENT	XVII
CHAPTER 1: SETTING UP AND EXPLORING GO	**1**
INTRODUCTION	2
RECIPE 1: INSTALLING GO AND CONFIGURING LINUX ENVIRONMENT	2
Situation	*2*
Practical Solution	*2*
RECIPE 2: EXPLORING GO MODULES AND PACKAGE MANAGEMENT	4
Situation	*4*
Practical Solution	*4*
RECIPE 3: CRAFTING YOUR FIRST PROGRAM WITH GO	5
Situation	*5*
Practical Solution	*5*
RECIPE 4: NAVIGATING GO WORKSPACE AND UNDERSTANDING FILE STRUCTURE	6
Situation	*7*
Practical Solution	*7*
RECIPE 5: EXPLORING FUNDAMENTAL GO SYNTAX AND DATA TYPES	8
Situation	*8*
Practical Solution	*9*
Arrays and Slices	9
Maps	10
Structs	10
RECIPE 6: MASTERING CONTROL STRUCTURES AND LOOPS	11
Situation	*11*
Practical Solution	*11*
RECIPE 7: EXPLORING FUNCTIONS AND METHODS IN GO	14
Situation	*14*
Practical Solution	*14*
RECIPE 8: POPULAR DEBUGGING TECHNIQUES IN GO WITH VS CODE	15
Situation	*15*
Practical Solution	*16*
Setting up for Debugging	16
Debugging Your Program	16
Logging and Diagnostics	16
SUMMARY	17
CHAPTER 2: ADVANCED GO FEATURES AND TECHNIQUES	**18**
INTRODUCTION	19
RECIPE 1: DIVING DEEP INTO POINTERS AND STRUCTS IN GO	19
Situation	*19*

Practical Solution......20
RECIPE 2: EXPLORING CLOSURES AND DEFER......21
   Situation......21
   Practical Solution......21
RECIPE 3: INTERFACE IMPLEMENTATION AND POLYMORPHISM......23
   Situation......23
   Practical Solution......23
RECIPE 4: CUSTOM ERROR HANDLING TECHNIQUES......25
   Situation......25
   Practical Solution......25
RECIPE 5: GOROUTINES AND CHANNELS......26
   Situation......26
   Practical Solution......27
RECIPE 6: UTILIZING GENERICS FOR FLEXIBLE CODE......28
   Situation......29
   Practical Solution......29
RECIPE 7: REFLECTION AND DATA MARSHALLING......30
   Situation......30
   Practical Solution......30
      Using Reflection......31
      Data Marshalling with JSON......32
RECIPE 8: WRITING AND EXECUTING UNIT TESTS......33
   Situation......33
   Practical Solution......33
SUMMARY......34

CHAPTER 3: FILE HANDLING AND DATA PROCESSING IN GO......36

INTRODUCTION......37
RECIPE 1: READING AND WRITING FILES......37
   Situation......37
   Practical Solution......38
      Defining a Book Structure......38
      Writing Books to a File......38
      Reading Books from a File......39
      Main Function......40
RECIPE 2: JSON AND XML HANDLING AND PROCESSING......41
   Situation......42
   Practical Solution......42
      Enhancing the Book Structure for XML......42
      Exporting Books to JSON and XML......42
      Importing Books from JSON and XML......43
RECIPE 3: UTILIZING REGULAR EXPRESSIONS FOR DATA PARSING......44
   Situation......45
   Practical Solution......45
RECIPE 4: PROCESSING CSV AND TEXT DATA EFFICIENTLY......47
   Situation......48
   Practical Solution......48
      Importing Books from a CSV File......48
      Exporting Books to a CSV File......49

RECIPE 5: BINARY DATA HANDLING AND ADVANCED FILE I/O 51
    Situation 51
    Practical Solution 51
        Reading a Binary File (Cover Image) 52
        Writing a Binary File (Cover Image) 52
        Integrating Cover Images with Book Entries 53
RECIPE 6: USING GO FOR TRANSFORMING DATA 54
    Situation 54
    Practical Solution 54
        Generating a Library Summary Report 54
        Exporting Data for Analysis 55
RECIPE 7: FILE SYSTEM OPERATIONS AND DIRECTORY MANAGEMENT 57
    Situation 57
    Practical Solution 57
        Creating Directories Based on Authors 57
        Cleaning Up Empty Directories 59
RECIPE 8: CREATING AND MANAGING TEMPORARY FILES AND DIRECTORIES 60
    Situation 60
    Practical Solution 61
        Creating a Temporary File 61
        Creating a Temporary Directory 61
        Using and Cleaning Up Temporary Resources 62
    SUMMARY 63

CHAPTER 4: BUILDING AND MANAGING GO APIS 65

    INTRODUCTION 66
    RECIPE 1: BUILDING A BASIC HTTP SERVER 66
    Situation 66
    Practical Solution 66
    RECIPE 2: HANDLING HTTP REQUESTS AND RESPONSES EFFECTIVELY 68
    Situation 68
    Practical Solution 68
        Implementing Route-Specific Handlers 68
        Parsing Query Parameters 69
        Setting up Routes 70
    RECIPE 3: DEVELOPING RESTFUL APIS 70
    Situation 70
    Practical Solution 70
        Defining the Book Resource Endpoints 71
        Implementing the Endpoints 71
        Routing 72
    RECIPE 4: IMPLEMENTING MIDDLEWARE FOR REQUEST PROCESSING 72
    Situation 73
    Practical Solution 73
        Defining a Middleware Function 73
        Applying Middleware to Handlers 73
        Building a Middleware Chain 74
    RECIPE 5: AUTHENTICATION MECHANISMS IN API DEVELOPMENT 75
    Situation 75
    Practical Solution 75

      Generating and Validating JWT Tokens 75
      User Authentication Endpoint 75
      Middleware for JWT Validation 77
  RECIPE 6: REAL-TIME COMMUNICATION WITH WEBSOCKETS **78**
    Situation *78*
    Practical Solution *79*
      Setting up a WebSocket Endpoint 79
      Integrating WebSocket Communication 80
      Client-Side Implementation 81
  RECIPE 7: VERSIONING APIS AND CREATING DOCUMENTATION FOR "LIBRAGO" APPLICATION **82**
    Situation *82*
    Practical Solution *82*
      Implementing API Versioning 82
      Creating API Documentation 82
  RECIPE 8: TESTING AND DEBUGGING API ENDPOINTS **84**
    Situation *84*
    Practical Solution *84*
      Unit Testing API Handlers 84
      Performance Testing 86
  SUMMARY **86**

CHAPTER 5: IMPLEMENTING RPC AND GRPC SERVICES IN GO 88

  INTRODUCTION **89**
  RECIPE 1: DEFINING PROTOBUFS AND SERVICE CONTRACTS **89**
    Situation *89*
    Practical Solution *90*
      RPC and gRPC Explained 90
      Defining Protobufs 90
  RECIPE 2: BUILDING ROBUST GRPC SERVERS **92**
    Situation *92*
    Practical Solution *92*
      Install gRPC for Go 92
      Implement the Server Interface 92
      Running the Server 94
  RECIPE 3: CRAFTING A GRPC CLIENT **94**
    Situation *94*
    Practical Solution *94*
      Initialize a gRPC Client Connection 94
      Making Requests to the Server 96
  RECIPE 4: HANDLING ERRORS IN GRPC SERVICES **96**
    Situation *96*
    Practical Solution *96*
      Standard gRPC Error Codes 96
      Returning Standard gRPC Errors 96
      Custom Error Metadata 97
      Client-Side Error Handling 97
  RECIPE 5: IMPLEMENTING STREAMING DATA WITH GRPC **98**
    Situation *99*
    Practical Solution *99*
      Server Streaming RPC 99
      Bidirectional Streaming RPC 100

Recipe 6: Ensuring gRPC Connection Security 101
- Situation 101
- Practical Solution 101
  - Generate SSL Certificates 101
  - Configure the gRPC Server for TLS 102
  - Configure the gRPC Client for TLS 102
Recipe 7: Adding Logging to gRPC Services 103
- Situation 103
- Practical Solution 103
  - Install Zap Logger 103
  - Setting up Zap Logger 104
  - Integrating Logging with gRPC Interceptors 104
  - Applying the Interceptor to the gRPC Server 105
Summary 106

CHAPTER 6: WEB SERVICES AND AUTOMATION USING GO 108

Introduction 109
Recipe 1: Implementing Templating and Static Assets 109
- Situation 109
- Practical Solution 109
  - Templating and Static Assets 110
  - Implementing Templating with Go's **html/template** 110
Recipe 2: Building and Consuming Web Services 112
- Situation 112
- Practical Solution 112
  - Create a RESTful API Endpoint 112
  - Consuming Web Services in Go 113
  - Handling JSON Data 114
Recipe 3: Effective Session Management in Web Apps 115
- Situation 115
- Practical Solution 115
  - Managing Sessions with Cookies 115
  - Token-Based Session Management 116
  - Session Storage 117
  - Security Considerations 117
Recipe 4: Automating Routine Tasks 117
- Situation 117
- Practical Solution 117
  - Creating a Simple Background Task Runner 117
  - Scheduling Tasks 118
Recipe 5: Scheduling Tasks with Cron Jobs 119
  - Setting up the Cron Package 119
  - Creating a Cron Job Scheduler 119
  - Cron Expressions 120
  - Error Handling and Job Inspection 120
  - Advanced Scheduling 121
Recipe 6: Integration with External APIs 121
  - Implementing External API Calls 121
  - Set up HTTP Client 121
  - Making a GET Request 122
  - Handling POST Requests 123

Security and Authentication 124
RECIPE 7: CREATING COMMAND-LINE TOOLS **124**
    Implementing a Basic CLI Tool in Go..124
    Using Cobra..125
SUMMARY 126

CHAPTER 7: BUILDING MICROSERVICES ARCHITECTURE USING GO 128

INTRODUCTION **129**
RECIPE 1: DESIGNING AND IMPLEMENTING A GO MICROSERVICE **129**
    Understanding Microservice Architecture *129*
    Practical Solution...*130*
        Define the Service Boundaries 130
        Set up the Go Microservice Project 130
        Implementing a Basic HTTP Server 130
        Define Domain Models and Business Logic..131
        Data Access Layer 132
        Microservices Communication...132
RECIPE 2: ACHIEVING EFFECTIVE INTER-SERVICE COMMUNICATION **132**
    Challenges in Inter-service Communication...*133*
    Practical Solution...*133*
        Implementing a REST Client with Go 133
        Implementing a Messaging Client 134
        Choosing the Right Pattern 135
RECIPE 3: IMPLEMENTING SERVICE DISCOVERY IN MICROSERVICES **136**
    Situation *136*
    Practical Solution...*136*
        Using a Service Registry 136
        Registering a Service with Consul in Go 136
        Discovering Services with Consul in Go...137
RECIPE 4: LOGGING AND MONITORING MICROSERVICES..**138**
    Scenario *138*
    Practical Solution...*139*
        Using Logrus with a Log Aggregator 139
        Monitoring with Prometheus and Grafana...139
        Visualizing Metrics with Grafana 140
RECIPE 5: CONTAINERIZING MICROSERVICES WITH DOCKER **140**
    Scenario *140*
    Practical Solution...*141*
        Installing Docker 141
        Verify the installation 141
        Creating a Dockerfile..141
        Building and Running Your Docker Container 142
        Run the container 142
RECIPE 6: ORCHESTRATING MICROSERVICES WITH KUBERNETES **143**
    Scenario *143*
    Setting up a Kubernetes Cluster *143*
        Install Minikube 143
        Start Minikube..143
        Verify Installation 144
    Deploying a Microservice to Kubernetes *144*
        Create a Deployment Configuration 144

Deploy Your Microservice 145
Expose Your Microservice 145
Accessing Your Service.. 145
Best Practices for Kubernetes.. 145
SUMMARY **146**

CHAPTER 8: STRENGTHENING DATABASE INTERACTIONS 147

INTRODUCTION 148
RECIPE 1: ESTABLISHING SQL DATABASE CONNECTIVITY IN GO 148
Scenario 148
Practical Solution.. 149
Install PostgreSQL Driver 149
Set up Database Connection 149
Understanding the Connection String 151
Testing the Connection 151
RECIPE 2: EXECUTING CRUD OPERATIONS WITH GO AND SQL 151
Scenario 151
Practical Solution.. 151
Create (Inserting Data) 151
Read (Querying Data) 152
Update (Modifying Data).. 153
Delete (Removing Data) 153
Best Practices... 154
RECIPE 3: LEVERAGING ORM TOOLS FOR DATABASE INTERACTION 154
Scenario 154
Practical Solution.. 154
Installing GORM... 154
Connecting to the Database 155
Defining a Model 155
Performing CRUD Operations.. 156
Benefits of Using an ORM... 156
RECIPE 4: ADVANCED TRANSACTION HANDLING AND CONCURRENCY 156
Scenario 157
Practical Solution.. 157
Using Transactions in Go... 157
Handling Concurrency 158
Best Practices... 158
RECIPE 5: WORKING WITH NOSQL DATABASES - MONGODB INTEGRATION 159
Scenario 159
Practical Solution.. 159
Setting up MongoDB in Go.. 159
Connecting to MongoDB.. 159
Defining a Model for User Reviews 160
Performing CRUD Operations.. 161
Best Practices... 161
RECIPE 6: EXECUTING ADVANCED QUERY TECHNIQUES FOR INSIGHTFUL DATA RETRIEVAL 162
Scenario 162
Practical Solution.. 162
SQL Window Functions in PostgreSQL.. 162
Aggregation Pipeline in MongoDB... 162
Combining SQL and NoSQL Queries for Data Insights 163

  Best Practices 163
 RECIPE 7: PERFORMING EFFECTIVE DATABASE MIGRATIONS **164**
  Scenario *164*
  Practical Solution *164*
   Choosing a Migration Tool 164
   Creating Migration Scripts 164
   Applying Migrations 165
   Rolling Back Migrations 165
   Best Practices 165
 RECIPE 8: IMPLEMENTING HIGH-PERFORMANCE DATABASE CACHING **165**
  Scenario *166*
  Practical Solution *166*
   Setting up Redis 166
   Integrating Redis with Go 166
   Caching Strategy for Frequently Accessed Data 167
   Best Practices 168
 SUMMARY **169**

CHAPTER 9: ENHANCING PERFORMANCE AND BEST PRACTICES IN GO 170

 INTRODUCTION **171**
 RECIPE 1: WRITING HIGH-PERFORMANCE GO CODE **171**
  Scenario *171*
  Practical Solution *172*
   Avoid Unnecessary Memory Allocations 172
   Leverage Concurrency for Parallel Processing 173
   Optimize Use of Interfaces and Reflection 174
   Best Practices 174
 RECIPE 2: PROFILING GO APPLICATIONS FOR PERFORMANCE TUNING **174**
  Scenario *174*
  Practical Solution *175*
   CPU Profiling 175
   Memory Profiling 176
   Block and Goroutine Profiling 176
   Best Practices 176
 RECIPE 3: ACHIEVING EFFICIENT MEMORY MANAGEMENT **177**
  Scenario *177*
  Practical Solution *177*
   Implementing Object Pooling 177
   Minimize Small Allocations 178
   Understand and Optimize Data Structures 178
   Leverage **sync.Pool** for Frequently Used Complex Objects 178
   Best Practices 178
 RECIPE 4: IMPLEMENTING SINGLETON FOR DATABASE CONNECTIONS **179**
  Scenario *179*
  Singleton Pattern Implementation *179*
   Define a Singleton Structure for Database Connection 179
   Using the Singleton Database Connection 180
   Benefits and Considerations 181
 RECIPE 5: MANAGING DEPENDENCIES AND GO MODULES EFFECTIVELY **181**
  Scenario *181*
  Practical Solution *181*

Initializing a New Module 181
Adding Dependencies 182
Upgrading and Downgrading Dependencies 182
Tidying Your Module 182
Vendoring Dependencies 182
Best Practices 182
SUMMARY **183**

CHAPTER 10: NETWORKING AND PROTOCOL HANDLING 184

INTRODUCTION **185**
RECIPE 1: BUILDING EFFICIENT HTTP CLIENTS **185**
   Scenario *185*
   Practical Solution *186*
      Use the **http.Client** with Custom Settings 186
      Making Concurrent Requests 187
      Best Practices 188
RECIPE 2: IMPLEMENTING FTP AND SSH CLIENTS **188**
   Scenario *188*
   Implementing an FTP Client *188*
      Example FTP Client for File Download 188
      Implementing an SSH Client 190
      Example SSH Client for Running Remote Commands 190
      Best Practices 191
RECIPE 3: DESIGNING AND IMPLEMENTING CUSTOM PROTOCOLS **192**
   Scenario *192*
   Practical Solution *192*
      Define the Protocol 192
      Server Setup 192
      Client Implementation 194
RECIPE 4: STANDARD WEBSOCKET PROGRAMMING IN GO **195**
   Scenario *195*
   Implementing a WebSocket Server in Go *195*
      Use the **gorilla/websocket** Package 195
      Create a Simple WebSocket Echo Server 195
      Implementing a WebSocket Client in Go 197
RECIPE 5: SECURE COMMUNICATIONS WITH TLS/SSL **199**
   Scenario *199*
   Implementing a TLS-secured HTTP Server *199*
      Generate TLS Certificates 199
      Create an HTTPS Server 200
      Securing WebSocket Connections with TLS 200
RECIPE 6: CONSTRUCTING A SIMPLE WEB SERVER FROM SCRATCH **201**
   Scenario *201*
   Practical Solution *201*
      Setting up the Server 201
      Running the Server 202
SUMMARY **202**
INDEX **204**
EPILOGUE **206**

Preface

The "Go Programming Cookbook" ensures Go programmers may confidently and effectively navigate the complex software development landscape. Both newcomers to the world of Go programming and seasoned professionals looking to sharpen their skills will find something of interest in this carefully written book. In its extensive chapters, the book provides a wealth of recipes, each one a workable answer to the many problems that programmers face on a regular basis.

This cookbook covers a wide range of topics, from the basics of Go syntax and core ideas to more advanced subjects like concurrency, networking, and microservices design. Building a Go development environment, learning the fundamentals of Go constructs, and mastering the art of Go Module dependency management are all covered in the first few chapters, which prepare readers for what's to come. To guarantee that readers can construct strong and maintainable programs, the next sections cover error handling, unit testing, and database interfaces.

The book really comes into its own when it comes to its in-depth examination of network programming; it covers topics like building HTTP clients, implementing FTP and SSH clients, and using WebSockets for real-time communication. To prepare developers to create safe, networked applications in a world where everything is always connected, it teaches them how to establish secure TLS/SSL communications, which is a fundamental component of security.

To help developers create Go code that runs efficiently, "Go Programming Cookbook" teaches them not only how to code, but also how to optimize performance, profile, and manage memory. In addition to providing practical solutions, the recipes educate readers on the concurrency model and design principles of Go, which helps them build an intuitive understanding of high-performance software development.

In this book you will learn how to:

- Get a solid grounding in programming by learning the syntax and concepts of Go.
- Explore concurrency with Goroutines and Channels to maximize Go's possibilities.
- Effortlessly handle intricate network programming jobs involving WebSockets and HTTP clients.
- Learn TLS/SSL inside and out to make your applications secure for transmitted sensitive information.
- Effectively manage data by integrating with SQL and NoSQL databases.
- Use Go Modules to have easier dependency management and build reproducibility.

- Make your Go code clean and easy to maintain by following design patterns and other best practices.
- Get the most out of your system by learning about memory management, benchmarking, and profiling.
- Create web servers and microservices from the ground up that are scalable and perform exceptionally well.
- Become an expert Go problem solver by learning practical answers to real-world issues.

GitforGits

Prerequisites

If you're serious about becoming an expert Go programmer, you need the "Go Programming Cookbook" more than anything else. It's a call to dive headfirst into the world of Go programming, try new things, and ultimately succeed. This book will show you how to become the best Go programmer you can be, whether you're interested in developing web apps, microservices, or simply want to streamline your development process.

Codes Usage

Are you in need of some helpful code examples to assist you in your programming and documentation? Look no further! Our book offers a wealth of supplemental material, including code examples and exercises.

Not only is this book here to aid you in getting your job done, but you have our permission to use the example code in your programs and documentation. However, please note that if you are reproducing a significant portion of the code, we do require you to contact us for permission.

But don't worry, using several chunks of code from this book in your program or answering a question by citing our book and quoting example code does not require permission. But if you do choose to give credit, an attribution typically includes the title, author, publisher, and ISBN. For example, "Go Programming Cookbook by Ian Taylor".

If you are unsure whether your intended use of the code examples falls under fair use or the permissions outlined above, please do not hesitate to reach out to us at support@gitforgits.com.

We are happy to assist and clarify any concerns.

Acknowledgement

I owe a tremendous debt of gratitude to GitforGits, for their unflagging enthusiasm and wise counsel throughout the entire process of writing this book. Their knowledge and careful editing helped make sure the piece was useful for people of all reading levels and comprehension skills. In addition, I'd like to thank everyone involved in the publishing process for their efforts in making this book a reality. Their efforts, from copyediting to advertising, made the project what it is today.

Finally, I'd like to express my gratitude to everyone who has shown me unconditional love and encouragement throughout my life. Their support was crucial to the completion of this book. I appreciate your help with this endeavour and your continued interest in my career.

Chapter 1: Setting up and Exploring Go

Introduction

In the first chapter, "Setting up and Exploring Go," we go on a trip to lay the groundwork for learning Go programming. This chapter is intended to walk you through the first steps of configuring a Go development environment on Linux, guaranteeing a seamless start to Go programming. We will go over how to install Go, configure the workspace, and choose the best tools and IDEs, with a special emphasis on VS Code because of its strong support and integration with Go.

Beyond the setup, this chapter goes into the fundamental notions that constitute the foundation of Go programming. You will understand Go's distinctive approach to variables, types, and control structures, allowing them to confidently construct their first Go programs. This chapter will take you step-by-step through the syntax and basic programming components of Go, covering everything from making a small program to learn about variables and control flow to more advanced topics like reusing code through package organization.

Error handling in Go, a fundamental component that distinguishes it from other languages, will be demonstrated via practical examples. You will discover the idiomatic way Go handles mistakes, ensuring that code is robust and reliable from the start. The chapter also explains the concept of unit testing in Go. It stresses the importance of testing in the Go ecosystem by showing you how to develop and execute simple tests, encouraging best practices from the start.

By the end of this chapter, you will not only have a working Go environment, but also a good understanding of Go's grammar, error handling, and testing frameworks. This foundation will prepare you for the next step into more sophisticated Go programming themes, ensuring you are ready to handle more complicated programming challenges using Go.

Recipe 1: Installing Go and Configuring Linux Environment

Situation

You are ready to embark on your Go programming journey but first need to install Go on your Linux system. This setup is your gateway to developing efficient and concurrent applications in Go.

Practical Solution

The journey begins by downloading the latest Go version. Head over to the Go official website, find the Linux package, and download it. Once the download is complete, the installation process can start.

To install Go, open your terminal and extract the downloaded archive into **/usr/local** with the following command. This step requires you to replace **$VERSION**, **$OS**, and **$ARCH** with the actual details corresponding to the Go version you've downloaded and your Linux system's architecture.

sudo tar -C /usr/local -xzf go$VERSION.$OS-$ARCH.tar.gz

After installing Go, it's crucial to set up your environment for Go development by adding Go's bin directory to your PATH. This enables you to execute Go commands from any terminal session. Add the following line to your **~/.profile** or **~/.bashrc**:

export PATH=$PATH:/usr/local/go/bin

To apply these changes, either log out and back in, or source your profile:

source ~/.profile

Verify Go is correctly installed by typing:

go version

This command should return the version of Go you've just installed.

Next, configuring your workspace is essential, even with Go modules simplifying dependency management and allowing you to work outside the traditional GOPATH. Create a directory named **go_workspace** in your home directory as a dedicated space for your Go projects. Inside **go_workspace**, you might set up a structure with directories for source code (**src**), compiled binaries (**bin**), and package objects (**pkg**).

For a robust development experience, installing Visual Studio Code (VS Code) is advisable. VS Code, complemented by Go extensions, offers an integrated coding, debugging, and testing environment. Install VS Code from its official website or through your Linux package manager. After installation, enhance VS Code for Go development by adding the Go extension available in the VS Code marketplace.

Example command to install VS Code via snap (Ubuntu)

sudo snap install code --classic

After VS Code is installed, launch it and navigate to the Extensions view by clicking on the square icon on the sidebar or pressing **Ctrl+Shift+X**. Search for the Go extension by the Go team and install it.

With Go installed, your environment configured, and your IDE set up, you are ready to tackle Go projects with efficiency and confidence. You can use this base as a starting point for all your Go development projects.

Recipe 2: Exploring Go Modules and Package Management

Situation

After setting up your Go environment, the next step is to understand how Go manages dependencies and organizes code. Go modules, introduced in Go 1.11, revolutionized package management in Go by enabling you to work outside the GOPATH, manage versioned dependencies, and improve project reproducibility. Suppose you are starting a new project or looking to migrate an existing project to use modules. In that case, it's essential to grasp how to create and manage Go modules for effective package management.

Practical Solution

To begin working with Go modules, you first need to initialize a new module in your project directory. Open your terminal, navigate to your project's root directory, and run the following command:

```
go mod init example.com/myproject
```

This command creates a new **go.mod** file in your project directory, declaring the current module's path, which is used by other projects to import packages from your module. The **go.mod** file also tracks your project's dependencies.

After initializing your module, you can start adding dependencies by simply importing them into your Go files. Go automatically adds direct imports to your **go.mod** file and downloads the necessary versions when you build or test your project. For instance, if you are using the popular **gorilla/mux** package for routing, import it in your code:

```
import "github.com/gorilla/mux"
```

Then, run your project or tests:

go run .

This command compiles and executes your project, automatically downloading and adding **gorilla/mux** to your **go.mod** file along with its version.

To explicitly add a dependency or to update its version, use the **go get** command:

go get github.com/gorilla/mux@v1.8.0

This command updates your **go.mod** to use version 1.8.0 of **gorilla/mux**, ensuring all your project's dependencies are precisely versioned and managed.

For projects with multiple dependencies, maintaining a tidy **go.mod** file becomes crucial. Use the **go mod tidy** command to remove unused dependencies and add any missing ones necessary for your current project's modules:

go mod tidy

This command ensures your **go.mod** file only contains the dependencies your project actually uses, keeping your module management clean and straightforward.

Recipe 3: Crafting Your First Program with Go

Situation

Now that you've set up your Go environment and familiarized yourself with Go modules and package management, it's time to write your very first Go program. The traditional "Hello, World!" program is a rite of passage for learning a new programming language. It's a simple yet powerful way to demonstrate the basic syntax and execution of code in Go. This program will print the message "Hello, World!" to the terminal, serving as a foundational step into Go programming.

Practical Solution

Begin by creating a new file named **hello.go** in your project directory. You can use any text editor or IDE of your choice, but ensure your development environment is properly configured for Go development, as learned in previous recipes.

Open **hello.go** and start by declaring the main package. In Go, every executable program begins with the **main** package:

```go
package main
```

Next, import the **fmt** package, which contains functions for formatting text, including printing to the console:

```go
import "fmt"
```

Next, define the **main** function. In Go, the **main** function is the entry point of the executable programs. It's where the execution of the program begins:

```go
func main() {

 fmt.Println("Hello, World!")

}
```

The **fmt.Println** function is used to print the string "Hello, World!" followed by a newline to the terminal.

Save your **hello.go** file and open a terminal in your project directory. Compile and run your program using the **go run** command:

```
go run hello.go
```

This command compiles your Go program and executes it, displaying the "Hello, World!" message in the terminal. If you see the message, congratulations! You've successfully written and executed your first Go program.

This simple program introduces several core concepts of Go programming:
- Every Go executable program starts with the **main** package.
- Importing packages to use in your program, like **fmt** for formatting and output.
- Defining functions, such as the **main** function, which is the entry point of the program.
- Calling functions from imported packages to perform actions, like printing to the console.

Recipe 4: Navigating Go Workspace and Understanding File Structure

Situation

Now that you know how to write a Go program, you may be asking how to best manage your Go projects and get around the workspace, particularly as they become more complex. A well-organized workspace and knowledge of Go's file structure are essential for the efficient creation and maintenance of Go applications. When dealing with modules, this is of utmost importance since it influences dependency management and application packaging.

Practical Solution

The rigid structure of the GOPATH workspace has become optional in the age of Go modules, giving you greater freedom in project organization. However, using a consistent framework for your projects can dramatically improve productivity and teamwork.

When starting a new Go project, first initialize a new module as previously described, using **go mod init** followed by your module path. This creates a **go.mod** file in your project's root directory, marking the start of your module. For instance, if your project is named **example**, your initial setup in the project directory might look like this:

mkdir example

cd example

go mod init example.com/example

Within your project, it's beneficial to organize your Go source files (***.go**) into packages. A package in Go is simply a directory within your project containing one or more **.go** files that provide a specific functionality. By convention, each directory under your project's root represents a separate package.

For a simple application, you might have a structure like this:

- /cmd: Contains your application's entry points. Each subdirectory inside cmd is named for an executable, and contains a main.go file where execution begins.
- /pkg: Houses reusable packages that can be imported by other applications or services. It's where the bulk of your logic might reside, structured into various packages based on functionality.
- /internal: Contains private application and library code. This code isn't intended to be imported by other applications.
- /api: Stores the API definitions for your service, often using Protocol Buffers.

Following is an example structure for an application named **example**:

```
/example

/cmd

/example

main.go # Entry point for the 'example' application

/pkg

/api # Package for API-related utilities

/db # Package for database interactions

/internal

/config # Internal package for configuration management

go.mod # Go module file

go.sum # Go checksum file
```

This structure isn't mandatory but following a convention similar to this can make it easier to navigate and maintain your projects, especially as they scale. It also helps other Go developers quickly understand the layout of your project. Remember, the **go.mod** file at the root of your project directory manages dependencies for the entire module, making it straightforward to build and package your application regardless of its internal directory structure.

Recipe 5: Exploring Fundamental Go Syntax and Data Types

Situation

Once you have your workspace organized and have written your first Go program, it's time to learn more about Go's syntax and the other data types it provides. Understanding these fundamentals is critical since they constitute the foundation of any Go application. Whether you are handling texts, doing numerical computations, or organizing data with arrays, slices, and maps, a good understanding of Go's syntax and data types will help you develop more efficient and effective code.

Practical Solution

Go's syntax is designed to be clean and concise, aiming to reduce clutter and make code easier to read and write. We will explore some of the fundamental aspects of Go's syntax and its primary data types.

- Variables and Constants: In Go, you declare variables with the **var** keyword, followed by the variable name and type. Go also supports type inference, where you don't need to explicitly mention the type of the variable.

var name string = "Go Programming Cookbook"

var version int = 1

// Using type inference

name := "Go Programming Cookbook"

version := 1

Constants are declared like variables but use the **const** keyword. Constants cannot be reassigned once set.

const LanguageName = "Go"

- Basic Data Types: Go supports basic data types like integers (**int**, **uint**, **int64**, **uint64** etc.), floating-point numbers (**float32**, **float64**), and booleans (**bool**). Strings in Go are immutable and defined with double quotes or backticks for raw strings.

var isActive bool = true

var score float64 = 99.5

var rawString string = `This is a raw string \n with no special escape sequences.`

- Composite Data Types: These include arrays, slices, maps, and structs. Arrays have a fixed size, while slices are dynamic. Maps provide a flexible way to store key-value pairs. Structs are used to define custom types with a collection of fields.

Arrays and Slices

```go
var days [7]string = [7]string{"Sunday", "Monday", "Tuesday", "Wednesday", "Thursday", "Friday", "Saturday"}

scores := []float64{9.0, 8.5, 9.5} // A slice of float64
```

Maps

```go
userInfo := map[string]string{"name": "John Doe", "occupation": "Software Developer"}
```

Structs

```go
type Book struct {
    Title string
    Author string
    Pages int
}

var myBook Book = Book{"Go Programming Cookbook", "Jane Doe", 300}
```

Control Structures: Go includes control structures such as **if**, **else**, **switch**, and loops (**for**). Go's **for** loop can act as a traditional for-loop, a while-loop, or a for-each loop.

```go
// Traditional for-loop
for i := 0; i < 10; i++ {
    fmt.Println(i)
}
// For-each range loop over a slice
for index, value := range scores {
    fmt.Printf("Score %d: %f\n", index, value)
```

}

All Go programs are built around these concepts, so you can confidently tackle varied programming jobs.

Recipe 6: Mastering Control Structures and Loops

Situation

After getting familiar with the basic syntax and data types, the next step in your Go programming journey involves mastering control structures and loops. Effective use of control structures such as **if**, **else**, **switch**, and loops like **for** is essential for adding logic and flow to your programs. Whether it's executing code based on certain conditions, iterating over collections, or repeatedly executing a block of code until a condition is met, understanding these constructs will significantly enhance your ability to solve problems and implement algorithms in Go.

Practical Solution

Go provides several control structures and loops that can handle a wide range of programming scenarios. We will explore how to use these effectively.

- If-Else Statements: In Go, **if** and **else** statements don't require parentheses around conditions but do require braces {} around the body. Go also supports initializing a statement as part of the **if** condition.

```
if num := 10; num%2 == 0 {

 fmt.Println(num, "is even")

} else {

 fmt.Println(num, "is odd")

}
```

- Switch Statements: **Switch** statements in Go evaluate cases from top to bottom, stopping when a case succeeds. Unlike some other languages, Go's **switch** does not need an explicit **break** for each case.

```go
switch day := 4; day {
case 1:
    fmt.Println("Monday")
case 2:
    fmt.Println("Tuesday")
case 3:
    fmt.Println("Wednesday")
case 4:
    fmt.Println("Thursday")
default:
    fmt.Println("It's the weekend")
}
```

- For Loops: The **for** loop is the only looping construct in Go and can be used in several ways. A traditional **for** loop includes initialization, condition, and post statements.

```go
for i := 0; i < 5; i++ {
    fmt.Println("Loop iteration", i)
}
```

It can also act as a **while** loop by omitting the initialization and post statements.

```go
i := 0
for i < 5 {
    fmt.Println("While-style loop iteration", i)
```

i++

}

Furthermore, the **for** loop can range over slices, arrays, strings, maps, and channels, making it extremely versatile.

fruits := []string{"apple", "banana", "mango"}

for index, fruit := range fruits {

fmt.Printf("Index: %d, Fruit: %s\n", index, fruit)

}

- Break and Continue: Within a loop, the **break** statement can be used to exit the loop early, while **continue** skips the current iteration and proceeds with the next one.

for i := 0; i < 10; i++ {

if i == 5 {

break // Exit the loop when i is 5

}

if i%2 == 0 {

continue // Skip the rest of the loop for even numbers

}

fmt.Println("Odd:", i)

}

As you gain experience, you will discover that these constructs are extremely useful for writing Go code that is not only efficient but also understandable and easy to maintain.

Recipe 7: Exploring Functions and Methods in Go

Situation

If you want to keep your Go codebase organized and efficient, you'll have to learn to reuse code blocks as you go along. Functions and methods in Go accomplish this objective by encapsulating reusable code into callable components. Functions are independent structures, whereas methods are functions coupled with a type. If you want to construct scalable and modular Go apps, you need to know how to define, use, and leverage methods and functions.

Practical Solution

Defining a function starts with the **func** keyword, followed by the function's name, parameter list, and the return type. Following is a simple example of a function that takes two integers as input and returns their sum:

```go
func add(x int, y int) int {

  return x + y

}
```

Go supports multiple return values from a function, which is particularly useful for returning a result and an error value from a function:

```go
func divide(x float64, y float64) (float64, error) {

  if y == 0.0 {

    return 0.0, errors.New("cannot divide by zero")

  }

  return x / y, nil

}
```

To call a function, simply use its name followed by arguments enclosed in parentheses:

```
sum := add(5, 7)

result, err := divide(10.0, 0.0)
```

Methods in Go are functions declared with a receiver argument, which is a type to which the method is attached. This allows the method to access the properties of the receiver type:

```
type Rectangle struct {
  Width float64
  Height float64
}
// Method with a receiver of type Rectangle
func (r Rectangle) Area() float64 {
  return r.Width * r.Height
}
```

You can call a method on a type instance (receiver) like this:

```
rect := Rectangle{Width: 10, Height: 5}
area := rect.Area()
```

Go also supports anonymous functions, which can be defined and called at the point of use, and functions as first-class citizens, allowing them to be passed as arguments to other functions, returned from functions, and assigned to variables.

Recipe 8: Popular Debugging Techniques in Go with VS Code

Situation

The more complicated your Go projects get, the more likely it is that you may encounter problems and defects. Debugging is an important skill for detecting and addressing these problems rapidly. Visual Studio Code (VS Code), with its extensive debugging capabilities specialized to Go, provides a smooth debugging experience. Learning how to use these tools can accelerate your development process and improve the quality of your work.

Practical Solution

To begin debugging Go code in VS Code, ensure you have the Go extension installed. This extension provides rich language support for Go, including debugging capabilities that integrate with the Delve debugger, a full-featured debugger for Go.

Setting up for Debugging

- Install Delve: If not already installed, you can install Delve using **go install**:

```
go install github.com/go-delve/delve/cmd/dlv@latest
```

- Configure launch.json: In VS Code, open your Go project and go to the Run and Debug view by clicking the play icon on the sidebar or pressing **Ctrl+Shift+D**. Click on "create a launch.json file" and select Go. VS Code will generate a **launch.json** file in the **.vscode** folder. This file tells VS Code how to launch and debug your application.

Debugging Your Program

- Breakpoints: Set breakpoints by clicking to the left of the line number in your Go code where you want execution to pause. Breakpoints can be conditional, pausing execution only when certain conditions are met.
- Start Debugging: With breakpoints set, start your debugging session by pressing **F5** or clicking the green play button in the Run and Debug view. Your program will start and pause at the first breakpoint.
- Inspect Variables: When execution is paused, you can hover over variables in your code to see their current values. The Debug pane also shows variables' values in the current scope.
- Step Through Code: Use the step over (**F10**), step into (**F11**), and step out (**Shift+F11**) commands to navigate through your code. This allows you to closely observe how your program's state changes.
- Watch Expressions: Add expressions to the Watch panel to evaluate their values in real-time as you step through the code.
- View Call Stack: The Call Stack panel shows the chain of function calls leading to the current execution point.

Logging and Diagnostics

In addition to interactive debugging, strategic logging can provide insights into your application's behavior. VS Code's integrated terminal makes it easy to run your application and view logs directly within the IDE.

You can improve your ability to find logic flaws, examine program state, and comprehend flow control in Go applications by becoming proficient with VS Code debugging techniques. This skill set is critical for creating reliable, error-free Go programs.

Summary

In this chapter, we took a foundational trip through the fundamentals of Go programming, designed for both newbies and experienced developers looking to solidify their knowledge of the language. Beginning with the setup of the Go environment on a Linux machine, we looked at the installation procedure, workspace configuration, and the critical function of Visual Studio Code (VS Code) as an IDE. This basic setup lays the framework for you to have the tools and environment you need to operate efficiently with Go.

We went into Go's package management with the introduction of Go modules, highlighting how to successfully create, manage, and use dependencies, representing a substantial transition from traditional GOPATH-based administration to a more modular and controllable approach. Our first journey into Go coding involved creating a "Hello, World!" program, which demonstrated the simplicity and elegance of Go syntax. As the exploration advanced, we gained a deeper knowledge of Go's data types, control structures, loops, functions, and procedures, with each part building on the previous one. These ideas are essential for organizing logic, managing data, and writing reusable and maintainable code.

The chapter concluded with an emphasis on debugging techniques in VS Code, demonstrating how to use breakpoints, inspect variables, and browse through code to locate and resolve errors quickly. This combination of theoretical understanding and actual application creates a comprehensive toolkit for managing Go projects. Throughout this voyage, you have earned a solid foundation in Go programming, including the ability to efficiently write, debug, and manage Go code, laying the groundwork for more advanced subjects and applications in the following chapters.

Chapter 2: Advanced Go Features and Techniques

Introduction

Moving beyond the fundamentals, we explore the more advanced aspects of Go programming in Chapter 2, "Advanced Go Features and Techniques," which enable you to create systems that are scalable, efficient, and robust. This chapter aims to shed light on Go's more complex capabilities, such as its extensive coverage of concurrency models, interface implementation and utility, error handling intricacies, and reflection and generics' powers. Each section is designed to solve real-world programming difficulties, providing solutions that maximize Go's capabilities.

We begin by looking at Go's strong concurrency paradigm, which uses goroutines and channels to conduct asynchronous tasks and communication, respectively. You will learn how to construct apps that can manage several activities at the same time, enhancing performance and responsiveness, using real-world examples. Following that, we will look at interfaces and type assertions, which are essential for designing Go code that is flexible and modular. Understanding how to establish and implement interfaces enables you to create systems with loosely linked components that are easier to maintain and enhance.

Error handling in Go takes a distinctive approach, with an emphasis on explicit checks over exceptions. This chapter teach methods for developing robust error handling mechanisms, such as establishing unique error types and packaging errors for better diagnostics. Furthermore, we investigate reflection and related applications, which allow programs to view and edit objects at runtime, providing dynamic capabilities that are especially valuable for serialization, deserialization, and working with generic data structures.

Finally, the addition of generics in Go 1.18 is a substantial shift in the language, allowing for more type-safe and reusable code. You will learn how to define and use generic functions and types by following examples and situations, eliminating redundancy and boosting code clarity.

This chapter teaches users how to tackle complicated programming scenarios, improving their ability to construct high-performance, maintainable, and scalable Go applications. This chapter not only broadens one's grasp of Go, but it also prepares you to apply these advanced concepts in real-world development context.

Recipe 1: Diving Deep into Pointers and Structs in Go

Situation

Understanding pointers and structs becomes increasingly important as you advance through the Go programming process. Pointers allow you to directly reference and manipulate memory locations, providing an efficient way to handle data and interact with Go's memory management. Structs, on the other hand, allow you to construct sophisticated data types that group variables under a single name, resulting in more ordered and comprehensible code. Pointers and structs constitute the foundation of Go's approach to data organizing and memory management, which is required for designing efficient and scalable applications.

Practical Solution

Pointers in Go offer a way to reference the memory address of a variable. Unlike some languages, Go does not support pointer arithmetic, making pointers safer and easier to use. To declare a pointer, you use the ***** (asterisk) followed by the type of the stored value. The **&** operator is used to find the address of a variable.

var a int = 58

var p *int = &a

fmt.Println("Address of a:", p) // Prints the memory address of a

fmt.Println("Value of a through pointer p:", *p) // Dereferencing p gives the value of a

Structs in Go allow you to compose together fields of different types into a single custom type. This is immensely useful for grouping related data together to form more logical and complex data structures.

type Person struct {

 Name string

 Age int

}

// Initializing a Person struct

person := Person{Name: "John Doe", Age: 30}

// Accessing struct fields

fmt.Println(person.Name) // Output: John Doe

You can use pointers with structs to reference and manipulate struct instances directly. This is particularly useful for functions that need to modify struct fields or when passing large structs to functions, as it avoids copying the entire struct.

```go
func birthday(p *Person) {
    p.Age += 1
}
// Calling birthday with a pointer to person
birthday(&person)
fmt.Println(person.Age) // Output: 31 (assuming previous age was 30)
```

If you want to define complicated types and make optimal use of memory in Go, you need to learn about and use pointers and structs. Your capacity to build efficient Go code, including the control and efficiency with which you handle data structures and memory, will be much improved after you master these ideas.

Recipe 2: Exploring Closures and Defer

Situation

Two powerful concepts that emerge are closures and the **defer** statement. Closures are a way to encapsulate data with functions, allowing the function to access variables from outside its immediate lexical scope. This feature is particularly useful for creating function generators or maintaining state across function calls. On the other hand, the **defer** statement postpones the execution of a function until the surrounding function returns, proving invaluable for resource management, such as closing files or releasing locks, ensuring these operations are performed reliably even in the face of errors.

Practical Solution

Closures in Go can be created by defining a function inside another function. The inner function has access to the variables defined in the outer function, allowing it to remember and manipulate these variables across multiple calls.

```go
func sequenceGenerator() func() int {
    i := 0
```

```go
    return func() int {
        i += 1
        return i
    }
}
nextNumber := sequenceGenerator()
fmt.Println(nextNumber()) // Output: 1
fmt.Println(nextNumber()) // Output: 2
```

The below sample program demonstrates a simple sequence generator, where each call to **nextNumber()** increments and returns a sequential number, showcasing how closures can maintain state.

The **defer** Statement in Go is used to ensure that a function call is executed later in a program's execution, typically for cleanup purposes. **defer** is often used where paired operations like open and close need to be executed together, enhancing code readability and safety.

```go
func readFile(filename string) {
    file, err := os.Open(filename)
    if err != nil {
        log.Fatalf("failed to open file: %s", err)
    }
    defer file.Close()
    // Process file
}
```

In the above sample program, **defer file.Close()** ensures that the open file is closed when the

readFile function completes, regardless of whether an error occurs during file processing. This pattern reduces the risk of resource leaks and makes the cleanup logic more concise and clear.

Recipe 3: Interface Implementation and Polymorphism

Situation

When creating code that is both flexible and modular, interfaces are crucial. In order to make types more decoupled and reusable, interfaces express a contract of behavior without describing how that behavior is realized. The implementation of shared methods allows a single function to communicate with different types in Go, achieving polymorphism. This is achieved through interfaces.

Practical Solution

To define an interface in Go, you use the **interface** keyword followed by a set of method signatures. Any type that implements all the methods in the interface is said to satisfy that interface, enabling it to be used in any context where the interface is expected.

```go
type Speaker interface {

 Speak() string

}

type Dog struct {

 Name string

}

func (d Dog) Speak() string {

 return "Woof! My name is " + d.Name

}

type Robot struct {
```

```
    Model string
}

func (r Robot) Speak() string {
    return "Beep boop. I am model " + r.Model
}
```

In the above sample program, both **Dog** and **Robot** types implement the **Speaker** interface by defining the **Speak** method. This allows instances of both **Dog** and **Robot** to be used in any context that requires a **Speaker**.

Polymorphism is demonstrated when you use the interface to write functions that can operate on any type that implements the interface. This is shown in the following function, which accepts a **Speaker** and calls its **Speak** method, regardless of the underlying concrete type.

```
func introduceSpeaker(s Speaker) {
    fmt.Println(s.Speak())
}

func main() {
    dog := Dog{Name: "Buddy"}
    robot := Robot{Model: "XJ-9"}
    introduceSpeaker(dog)   // Output: Woof! My name is Buddy
    introduceSpeaker(robot) // Output: Beep boop. I am model XJ-9
}
```

The **introduceSpeaker** function works with any **Speaker**, showcasing polymorphism in action. This approach significantly enhances the flexibility and modularity of your Go programs, allowing you to design components that are easy to extend and maintain.

Recipe 4: Custom Error Handling Techniques

Situation

To handle errors in a novel way, Go treats them as mutable and verifiable values. The technique allows for the implementation of advanced error handling strategies and promotes explicit error checking. The ability to build descriptive error categories and apply structured error recovery patterns is a significant strength of custom error handling. If you are developing Go apps, this recipe will show you how to improve error handling by defining and using custom errors.

Practical Solution

Go provides the **error** interface, which is the conventional interface for representing an error condition, with the nil value representing no error. For custom error handling, you can define types that implement this interface, allowing you to add context-specific information to your errors.

```go
type MyError struct {

 Msg string

 Code int

}

func (e *MyError) Error() string {

 return fmt.Sprintf("Code %d: %s", e.Code, e.Msg)

}

// Function that returns an error

func myFunction() error {

 // Error condition

 return &MyError{Msg: "Something went wrong", Code: 404}

}
```

In the above sample program, **MyError** is a custom error type that includes an error message and a code. By implementing the **Error()** method, **MyError** satisfies the **error** interface, allowing it to be used wherever **error** values are expected.

Using custom errors enables you to handle errors more precisely. You can use type assertions or type switches to differentiate between error types and implement logic based on specific error characteristics.

```
err := myFunction()

if err != nil {

switch e := err.(type) {

case *MyError:

fmt.Println("Custom error occurred:", e)

default:

fmt.Println("Generic error:", err)

}

}
```

Not only does this method of managing mistakes make your code more robust, but it also enhances readability and maintainability by giving clear information about fault conditions. To help calling functions make educated judgments about how to deal with various kinds of problems, custom errors provide a systematic mechanism to convey error information up the call stack.

Recipe 5: Goroutines and Channels

Situation

Think about the challenge of developing a system that can handle massive amounts of data coming from several sources all at once. It may not be the most efficient use of time to do this in consecutive order, particularly if the data sets are unrelated. To get the most out of your resources and cut down on processing time, you need a mechanism to run various tasks simultaneously. Achieving efficient management of these concurrent processes is the real problem, as it is essential to process data without delays or race situations.

Practical Solution

Go's concurrency model, built around goroutines and channels, offers a powerful solution to this problem. Goroutines are lightweight threads managed by the Go runtime, allowing you to perform concurrent operations with minimal overhead. Channels provide a way for goroutines to communicate, synchronizing execution and safely sharing data.

To tackle the problem, you can create a goroutine for processing each data set. This allows each data set to be processed independently and concurrently. Channels can be used to collect results from each goroutine or to control access to shared resources, preventing race conditions.

Following is a basic implementation:

```go
package main

import (

"fmt"

"sync"

)

// Simulate processing data

func processData(data int, wg *sync.WaitGroup, results chan<- int) {

defer wg.Done()

// Simulate data processing with a simple operation

result := data * 2

results <- result

}

func main() {

var wg sync.WaitGroup
```

```go
dataSets := []int{1, 2, 3, 4, 5}

results := make(chan int, len(dataSets))

for _, data := range dataSets {

wg.Add(1)

go processData(data, &wg, results)

}

// Close the results channel once all goroutines have finished

go func() {

wg.Wait()

close(results)

}()

// Collect results

for result := range results {

fmt.Println(result)

}

}
```

In the above sample program, **processData** is a function that simulates processing data and then sends the result to a channel. A **sync.WaitGroup** is used to wait for all goroutines to finish their work. Each data set from **dataSets** is processed in a separate goroutine, allowing concurrent processing. Results are sent to the **results** channel, which are then collected and printed in the main goroutine.

Recipe 6: Utilizing Generics for Flexible Code

Situation

You are developing a library function that needs to be versatile enough to work with various data types. Previously, you might have resorted to using interfaces and type assertions, which can be cumbersome and error-prone, especially when dealing with multiple types. The challenge is to create a function that can accept any data type as its input while maintaining type safety and minimizing runtime overhead. This function should be able to perform a common operation, like sorting or filtering, without knowing the specific type of its arguments in advance.

Practical Solution

With the introduction of generics in Go 1.18, you can now create functions that are type-agnostic yet type-safe. Generics allow you to write functions, types, and methods that can operate on many different data types while still being checked at compile time. This is achieved by using type parameters, which are placeholders for the actual types that will be used when the function is called.

Given below is how you can implement a generic function that filters elements from any slice based on a user-defined criteria:

```go
package main

import "fmt"

// Filter takes a slice of any type and a function that defines the filtering criteria.
func Filter[T any](slice []T, criteria func(T) bool) []T {
    var result []T
    for _, v := range slice {
        if criteria(v) {
            result = append(result, v)
        }
    }
    return result
}
```

```go
func main() {
    // Example usage with a slice of integers
    ints := []int{1, 2, 3, 4, 5}
    even := Filter(ints, func(n int) bool { return n%2 == 0 })
    fmt.Println(even) // Output: [2 4]

    // Example usage with a slice of strings
    strings := []string{"apple", "banana", "cherry", "date"}
    withA := Filter(strings, func(s string) bool { return s[0] == 'a' })
    fmt.Println(withA) // Output: [apple banana]
}
```

In the above sample program, the **Filter** function is defined with a type parameter **[T any]**, indicating it can operate on a slice of any type. The function takes a slice and a **criteria** function as arguments. The **criteria** function itself is a generic function that accepts a value of the same type as the slice's elements and returns a **bool** indicating whether the element meets the criteria. This implementation allows **Filter** to be used with slices of any type, demonstrating the power and flexibility of generics for creating reusable and type-safe code.

Recipe 7: Reflection and Data Marshalling

Situation

Create a system that dynamically manipulates objects without compile-time type knowledge. When working with data types that originate from diverse places, such JSON from REST APIs, this happens frequently. Converting these items to and from a serialized format efficiently, as well as allowing for on-the-fly inspection and modification, are challenges that must be addressed in code.

Practical Solution

Go's **reflect** package and its support for data marshalling come into play for addressing such dynamic data handling needs. Reflection provides the ability to inspect and manipulate objects at runtime, identifying their types, fields, methods, and more. Data marshalling, particularly with JSON, allows for the conversion of Go values to and from JSON, making it easy to work with data from web services.

Using Reflection

Reflection can be used to inspect the type of variables and to dynamically access and modify their values. Following is a simple example of using reflection to inspect a variable's type:

```go
package main

import (
    "fmt"
    "reflect"
)

func inspectVariable(variable interface{}) {
    t := reflect.TypeOf(variable)
    v := reflect.ValueOf(variable)
    fmt.Println("Type:", t)
    fmt.Println("Value:", v)
}

func main() {
    myVar := 42
    inspectVariable(myVar)
}
```

This code demonstrates how to obtain and print the type and value of any variable passed to **inspectVariable**. While simple, this showcases reflection's power to work with unknown types.

Data Marshalling with JSON

For converting Go objects to JSON and vice versa, the **encoding/json** package is used. This is crucial for applications that consume or produce JSON, such as web services.

```go
package main

import (
    "encoding/json"
    "fmt"
    "log"
)

type Person struct {
    Name string `json:"name"`
    Age  int    `json:"age"`
}

func main() {
    // Marshal a Person object to JSON
    p := Person{Name: "John Doe", Age: 30}
    jsonData, err := json.Marshal(p)
    if err != nil {
        log.Fatalf("Error marshalling to JSON: %s", err)
    }
    fmt.Println(string(jsonData))

    // Unmarshal JSON to a Person object
```

```
    var p2 Person

    err := json.Unmarshal(jsonData, &p2)

    if err != nil {

    log.Fatalf("Error unmarshalling JSON: %s", err)

    }

    fmt.Println(p2)

}
```

By mapping fields in a Person struct in Go to keys in JSON, this example shows how to do the reverse conversion. Applications may process and transmit data with superior flexibility and performance using a robust toolkit for dynamic data handling in Go that combines reflection with JSON marshalling/unmarshalling.

Recipe 8: Writing and Executing Unit Tests

Situation

You are responsible for the upkeep of a sizable Go application as part of a development team. The team has recently been working hard to improve the application's dependability after discovering multiple problems that made it into production. The next step is to build a robust set of unit tests that can detect these issues at an early stage of development. Unfortunately, the team is still learning the ropes of Go's testing framework and could use any pointers on how to construct and run comprehensive unit tests for the app's features.

Practical Solution

Go provides a built-in testing framework that simplifies the process of writing and running unit tests. Tests in Go are written in the same package as the code they test and are placed in files named with the **_test.go** suffix. The **testing** package supplies the necessary tools for writing tests, including functions for marking a test as failed and logging test output.

To write a unit test, you define a function in a **_test.go** file with a name beginning with **Test**, followed by a description of the function being tested. This function takes a single argument, **t *testing.T**, which is used for reporting test failures and logging.

Given below is an example of a simple unit test for a function **Add** that sums two integers:

```go
package mathops

import "testing"

// Function to be tested
func Add(a, b int) int {
    return a + b
}

// TestAdd tests the Add function
func TestAdd(t *testing.T) {
    result := Add(1, 2)
    expected := 3
    if result != expected {
        t.Errorf("Add(1, 2) = %d; want %d", result, expected)
    }
}
```

To execute your tests, use the **go test** command in the terminal within the directory of your package. This command automatically identifies any **_test.go** files, runs the tests defined within them, and outputs the results. For more detailed output, including the results of each individual test, you can run **go test -v**.

Go's testing framework also supports benchmark tests for performance testing, table-driven tests for testing functions across various inputs, and setup/teardown logic for preparing necessary state or resources before tests and cleaning up afterward.

Summary

This chapter has provided us with a better understanding and practical skills for maximizing the potential of Go programming. We investigated the intricate workings of pointers and structs, discovering how they facilitate efficient data manipulation and organizing, laying the framework for more complicated data structures. The investigation of advanced functions shed light on closures and the defer statement, demonstrating their vital roles in managing scope, state, and ensuring resources are handled gracefully, hence improving code dependability and maintainability.

The adventure continued with a detailed analysis of interfaces and polymorphism, which revealed Go's type system's ability to construct flexible and modular programs. Custom error handling approaches were introduced, enabling options for creating more descriptive and actionable errors, which are critical when developing robust applications. The chapter then went over Go's concurrency paradigm, including goroutines and channels, demonstrating how to build highly concurrent and efficient programs. The advent of generics was a huge step forward in Go, allowing you to construct type-agnostic yet type-safe code, simplifying and enriching the development process.

Finally, we learned the crucial components of reflection and data marshalling, which enable dynamic data processing and seamless interaction with serialized data types. The chapter concludes by emphasizing the necessity of unit testing in Go, outlining strategies for developing and running tests to assure code quality and stability. Throughout this chapter, the combination of theory and practical examples has not only increased our comprehension but also illustrated the use of Go's advanced capabilities, preparing us to face complex programming challenges with confidence and expertise.

Chapter 3: File Handling and Data Processing in Go

Introduction

The goal of this chapter is to provide you with the background you need to understand and implement advanced data processing techniques and efficient file operations in Go. This chapter delves into the fundamental responsibilities of reading from and writing to files, demonstrating Go's built-in support for a variety of file formats and data streams. Through a series of carefully constructed recipes, we will investigate several scenarios ranging from basic text file interactions to more complex activities such as working with JSON, XML, and CSV formats, addressing frequent and advanced use cases seen in real-world applications.

The voyage begins with an introduction to file opening, reading, and writing, which lays the groundwork for more advanced data handling activities. We will look at how to effectively process huge files, implement file scanning, and manage file permissions to ensure you understand the subtleties of Go's file system operations. The focus will next transition to serialization and deserialization techniques, which are essential for working with structured data types. You will learn how to marshal and unmarshal data in JSON and XML, allowing for easy data interchange between Go programs and external services. The chapter will also teach how to handle CSV files, which are commonly used in data-driven applications, as well as ways for parsing and producing CSV data using Go.

Beyond file manipulation, this chapter will delve into sophisticated data processing ideas, such as regular expressions for data validation and searching, as well as binary data handling approaches tailored to specialized demands such as image processing or bespoke serialization formats. Each recipe addresses a specific task while simultaneously reinforcing best practices for error management, performance optimization, and producing clean, maintainable code.

After finishing this chapter, you will be well-versed in Go's data processing and file handling capabilities, with the tools you need to solve a variety of problems. Whether dealing with basic text files or sophisticated structured data, the skills learned here will be invaluable in designing solid, efficient Go applications that can successfully manage and analyze data.

Recipe 1: Reading and Writing Files

We will consider developing a Go application centered around a personal library management system. This system, dubbed "LibraGo," will help users manage their collection of books, including operations like adding new books, listing existing ones, and saving or retrieving book details from a file.

Situation

In the "LibraGo" application, we need a reliable way to persist information about books in the library. The application should allow users to save new entries to a file and retrieve them upon request. This functionality requires implementing efficient and robust file reading and writing operations in Go, ensuring data integrity and ease of access.

Practical Solution

To address this requirement, we will start by defining a simple structure to represent a book and then implement functions to write book details to a file and read them back.

Defining a Book Structure

```go
package main

import (
    "bufio"
    "encoding/json"
    "fmt"
    "os"
)

type Book struct {
    Title  string `json:"title"`
    Author string `json:"author"`
    Pages  int    `json:"pages"`
}
```

Writing Books to a File

To persist book details, we will serialize our **Book** objects into JSON format and write them to a file. This approach makes it easier to extend our data model and interact with other systems in the future.

```go
func SaveBooks(filename string, books []Book) error {
    file, err := os.Create(filename)
```

```go
if err != nil {

return err

}

defer file.Close()

writer := bufio.NewWriter(file)

for _, book := range books {

jsonData, err := json.Marshal(book)

if err != nil {

return err

}

_, err = writer.WriteString(string(jsonData) + "\n")

if err != nil {

return err

}

}

return writer.Flush()

}
```

Reading Books from a File

To retrieve the saved books, we will read the file line by line, deserializing each line from JSON back into a **Book** object.

```go
func LoadBooks(filename string) ([]Book, error) {
```

```go
var books []Book

file, err := os.Open(filename)

if err != nil {

return nil, err

}

defer file.Close()

scanner := bufio.NewScanner(file)

for scanner.Scan() {

var book Book

if err := json.Unmarshal([]byte(scanner.Text()), &book); err != nil {

return nil, err

}

books = append(books, book)

}

return books, scanner.Err()

}
```

Main Function

Given below is how you might use these functions in the main part of your application:

```go
func main() {

books := []Book{

{"The Go Programming Language", "Alan A. A. Donovan", 380},
```

```go
        {"Go in Action", "William Kennedy", 300},
    }

    filename := "books.json"

    // Save books to file
    if err := SaveBooks(filename, books); err != nil {
        fmt.Println("Error saving books:", err)
        return
    }

    // Load books from file
    loadedBooks, err := LoadBooks(filename)
    if err != nil {
        fmt.Println("Error loading books:", err)
        return
    }

    fmt.Println("Loaded Books:", loadedBooks)
}
```

This solution outlines the basic operations for reading and writing files in the "LibraGo" application, ensuring that users can easily manage their library data. The application's data persistence has been firmly established through the utilization of Go's inherent capabilities for JSON serialization and file operations.

Recipe 2: JSON and XML Handling and Processing

Situation

The "LibraGo" app must be able to import and export book details in two different formats: JSON and XML. To support this functionality, the app needs to be able to handle these formats in a variety of ways, so users may easily communicate with other library management systems or data sources that use JSON or XML.

Practical Solution

Go provides robust support for both JSON and XML handling through the **encoding/json** and **encoding/xml** packages, respectively. We will leverage these to implement functions in "LibraGo" for parsing and generating data in these formats.

Enhancing the Book Structure for XML

First, we will add XML annotations to our **Book** struct, ensuring it can be properly serialized and deserialized from XML.

```go
type Book struct {
  Title string `json:"title" xml:"title"`
  Author string `json:"author" xml:"author"`
  Pages int `json:"pages" xml:"pages"`
}

// For XML, we often work with a wrapper type to represent a collection of books.
type Library struct {
  Books []Book `xml:"book"`
}
```

Exporting Books to JSON and XML

Next, we implement functions to serialize a slice of **Book** objects into JSON and XML. While the JSON functionality was covered in the previous recipe, following is how you might add XML serialization:

```go
func ExportBooksToXML(books []Book) (string, error) {

    library := Library{Books: books}

    xmlData, err := xml.MarshalIndent(library, "", "  ")

    if err != nil {

    return "", err

    }

    return string(xmlData), nil

}
```

Importing Books from JSON and XML

For importing, we will parse data from JSON and XML back into our **Book** or **Library** structs. The JSON importing was demonstrated earlier; below is an example for XML:

```go
func ImportBooksFromXML(xmlData string) ([]Book, error) {

    var library Library

    err := xml.Unmarshal([]byte(xmlData), &library)

    if err != nil {

    return nil, err

    }

    return library.Books, nil

}
```

These functionalities allow "LibraGo" to interact with data in both JSON and XML formats, enhancing its versatility.

Given below is a brief illustration of using these new capabilities:

```go
func main() {

    // Assuming books slice is already defined and populated

    xmlOutput, err := ExportBooksToXML(books)

    if err != nil {

        fmt.Println("Error exporting books to XML:", err)

        return

    }

    fmt.Println("XML Output:", xmlOutput)

    // Simulate importing books from XML

    importedBooks, err := ImportBooksFromXML(xmlOutput)

    if err != nil {

        fmt.Println("Error importing books from XML:", err)

        return

    }

    fmt.Println("Imported Books:", importedBooks)

}
```

As a result of these developments, "LibraGo" can now manage book data within its own ecosystem and even facilitate external data sharing. To guarantee data interoperability and flexibility across many platforms and services, modern programs must be able to handle and interpret JSON and XML.

Recipe 3: Utilizing Regular Expressions for Data Parsing

Situation

"LibraGo" users have access to a plain text file that lists books in a specific format, e.g., "Title: [Book Title], Author: [Author Name], Pages: [Number of Pages]". The challenge is to develop a function within "LibraGo" that can parse this text file, extract book details following this pattern, and convert them into **Book** struct instances for further processing and inclusion in the user's library.

Practical Solution

To tackle this challenge, we will leverage Go's **regexp** package, which provides robust support for regular expressions, allowing us to define a pattern that matches the book details in the text and extract the necessary information.

First, define a regular expression that captures the format of the book listings in the text file:

import (

"bufio"

"fmt"

"os"

"regexp"

)

var bookDetailsPattern = regexp.MustCompile(`Title: (.+), Author: (.+), Pages: (\d+)`)

Next, implement a function that reads the text file line by line, applies the regular expression to extract book details, and constructs **Book** instances from these details:

func ParseBooksFromFile(filename string) ([]Book, error) {

file, err := os.Open(filename)

if err != nil {

return nil, err

}

```go
defer file.Close()

var books []Book

scanner := bufio.NewScanner(file)

for scanner.Scan() {

    matches := bookDetailsPattern.FindStringSubmatch(scanner.Text())

    if matches != nil && len(matches) == 4 {

        title := matches[1]

        author := matches[2]

        pages, err := strconv.Atoi(matches[3])

        if err != nil {

            // Log error and continue parsing the rest of the file

            fmt.Printf("Invalid page number for book '%s': %s\n", title, err)

            continue

        }

        books = append(books, Book{Title: title, Author: author, Pages: pages})

    }

}

if err := scanner.Err(); err != nil {

    return nil, err

}

return books, nil
```

}

This function uses **bufio.Scanner** to read the file line by line, applying the **bookDetailsPattern** regular expression to each line. The **FindStringSubmatch** method extracts the title, author, and page count from each matching line. These extracted values are then used to create **Book** instances, which are appended to a slice that is returned at the end.

To use this parsing function in "LibraGo," simply call it with the path to the text file containing the book listings:

```go
func main() {

    filename := "book_listings.txt"

    books, err := ParseBooksFromFile(filename)

    if err != nil {

        fmt.Println("Error parsing books from file:", err)

        return

    }

    for _, book := range books {

        fmt.Printf("Parsed Book: %+v\n", book)

    }

}
```

This recipe showcases the usefulness of regular expressions for Go developers, particularly when working with pattern matching or extracting data from unstructured text. Because of this method, "LibraGo" is now better able to import data from informal sources by effectively parsing book details.

Recipe 4: Processing CSV and Text Data Efficiently

Situation

"LibraGo" must now incorporate a feature to import book collections from CSV files, where each row represents a book with fields for title, author, and page count. Similarly, the application should allow exporting the user's book collection to a CSV file.

Practical Solution

Go's **encoding/csv** package provides comprehensive support for reading and writing CSV data, making it straightforward to implement CSV processing in "LibraGo".

Following is how to create functions to import and export book collections using CSV format:

Importing Books from a CSV File

To read book details from a CSV file and convert them into a slice of **Book** structs, you can use the following approach:

```go
import (

"encoding/csv"

"os"

"strconv"

)

func ImportBooksFromCSV(filename string) ([]Book, error) {

file, err := os.Open(filename)

if err != nil {

return nil, err

}

defer file.Close()

reader := csv.NewReader(file)

records, err := reader.ReadAll()
```

```go
    if err != nil {
        return nil, err
    }
    var books []Book
    for _, record := range records {
        pages, err := strconv.Atoi(record[2])
        if err != nil {
            // Handle error
            continue
        }
        books = append(books, Book{
            Title:  record[0],
            Author: record[1],
            Pages:  pages,
        })
    }
    return books, nil
}
```

Exporting Books to a CSV File

Conversely, to write a slice of **Book** structs to a CSV file, the following function outlines a practical method:

```go
func ExportBooksToCSV(filename string, books []Book) error {
    file, err := os.Create(filename)
    if err != nil {
        return err
    }
    defer file.Close()
    writer := csv.NewWriter(file)
    defer writer.Flush()
    for _, book := range books {
        record := []string{book.Title, book.Author, strconv.Itoa(book.Pages)}
        if err := writer.Write(record); err != nil {
            // Handle error
            return err
        }
    }
    return nil
}
```

These functionalities allow "LibraGo" to interact with CSV data, making it possible to import and export book collections efficiently. Given below is how you might integrate these functions into the main application flow:

```go
func main() {
    filename := "books.csv"
```

```go
// Assume books is populated with Book structs
if err := ExportBooksToCSV(filename, books); err != nil {
    fmt.Printf("Failed to export books to CSV: %s\n", err)
}

importedBooks, err := ImportBooksFromCSV(filename)
if err != nil {
    fmt.Printf("Failed to import books from CSV: %s\n", err)
} else {
    fmt.Println("Imported Books:", importedBooks)
}
```

This functionality not only facilitates data exchange with external sources but also empowers users to maintain their libraries with familiar tools like spreadsheets.

Recipe 5: Binary Data Handling and Advanced File I/O

Situation

"LibraGo" users want to associate cover images with their books, requiring the application to handle binary data efficiently. This feature involves reading binary files (images) from disk, associating them with the corresponding book entries, and providing functionality to update or retrieve these images. The challenge lies in performing these operations in a way that is both efficient and maintains the integrity of the binary data.

Practical Solution

Handling binary data in Go can be achieved through the **os** and **io** packages, which provide functions for advanced file operations. Given below is how to implement reading and writing binary files, using cover images as an example:

Reading a Binary File (Cover Image)

To read a cover image from disk and store it as a byte slice, use the following approach:

```go
import (
    "io/ioutil"
    "os"
)

func ReadCoverImage(filePath string) ([]byte, error) {
    file, err := os.Open(filePath)
    if err != nil {
        return nil, err
    }
    defer file.Close()
    imageData, err := ioutil.ReadAll(file)
    if err != nil {
        return nil, err
    }
    return imageData, nil
}
```

Writing a Binary File (Cover Image)

To write a cover image back to disk, either after modification or to save a new image, you can use this method:

```go
func WriteCoverImage(filePath string, data []byte) error {
    return ioutil.WriteFile(filePath, data, 0644)
}
```

Integrating Cover Images with Book Entries

To associate cover images with books, you might extend the **Book** struct to include a field for the image data or a reference to the image file:

```go
type Book struct {
    Title string
    Author string
    Pages int
    CoverPath string // Path to cover image file
}
```

Then, you can modify the **LibraGo** application to handle cover images when adding or updating book entries, ensuring each book can be associated with its cover image.

Integrating image handling into the main application flow might look like this:

```go
func main() {
    coverImagePath := "path/to/cover.jpg"

    // Reading cover image
    coverImage, err := ReadCoverImage(coverImagePath)
    if err != nil {
        fmt.Printf("Failed to read cover image: %s\n", err)
```

```go
    return
}

// Assuming a book needs its cover image updated
if err := WriteCoverImage(coverImagePath, coverImage); err != nil {
    fmt.Printf("Failed to write cover image: %s\n", err)
}
}
```

This capability allows users to maintain a more comprehensive and visually enriched library, making the application a more powerful tool for library management.

Recipe 6: Using Go for Transforming Data

Situation

Now that "LibraGo" is complete, it needs features to change the library data for new uses. As an example, a user may wish to compile a report detailing their library's contents, including the overall number of volumes, the average number of pages per book, and a breakdown by author. Users should also be aware that data analysis tools may need them to export library data in a specific format. The difficulty lies in the ease and adaptability of implementing these data transformation procedures.

Practical Solution

Go's strong support for data manipulation, coupled with its standard library, makes it well-suited for these tasks. We can leverage Go's slice and map functionalities, along with sorting and custom comparison functions, to transform and aggregate library data.

Generating a Library Summary Report

To create a summary report, we might aggregate data to count books, calculate average pages, and organize books by author.

```go
import (
```

```go
    "fmt"
    "sort"
)
func GenerateLibrarySummary(books []Book) {
    fmt.Printf("Total Books: %d\n", len(books))
    var totalPages int
    booksByAuthor := make(map[string][]Book)
    for _, book := range books {
        totalPages += book.Pages
        booksByAuthor[book.Author] = append(booksByAuthor[book.Author], book)
    }
    avgPages := float64(totalPages) / float64(len(books))
    fmt.Printf("Average Pages per Book: %.2f\n", avgPages)
    for author, books := range booksByAuthor {
        fmt.Printf("%s has %d books\n", author, len(books))
    }
}
```

Exporting Data for Analysis

For exporting data in a format suitable for analysis, we might convert our library data into a simple CSV format that can be easily imported into data analysis tools.

```go
func ExportLibraryDataForAnalysis(filename string, books []Book) error {
```

```go
file, err := os.Create(filename)
if err != nil {
    return err
}
defer file.Close()
writer := csv.NewWriter(file)
defer writer.Flush()
// Write header
if err := writer.Write([]string{"Title", "Author", "Pages"}); err != nil {
    return err
}
// Write book data
for _, book := range books {
    if err := writer.Write([]string{book.Title, book.Author, strconv.Itoa(book.Pages)}); err != nil {
        return err
    }
}
return nil
}
```

Incorporating these functionalities into the main application allows users to not only manage but also analyze their library in versatile ways.

```go
func main() {
    // Assuming books is a slice of Book populated with the user's library data
    GenerateLibrarySummary(books)
    if err := ExportLibraryDataForAnalysis("library_analysis.csv", books); err != nil {
        fmt.Printf("Failed to export library data for analysis: %s\n", err)
    }
}
```

The addition of these data processing features transforms "LibraGo" into a platform for analysis and insights in addition to a tool for library administration. Aligning with the larger goal of making "LibraGo" a complete library solution, this upgrade allows users to extract valuable information from their collections.

Recipe 7: File System Operations and Directory Management

Situation

Users of "LibraGo" are accumulating digital book files and cover images, leading to cluttered and disorganized directories. They need functionality within "LibraGo" to automatically organize these files into structured directories based on certain criteria, such as author names or genres. Additionally, the application should be capable of performing routine file system operations like creating new directories, moving files between directories, and cleaning up empty directories.

Practical Solution

Go's **os** and **path/filepath** packages provide comprehensive support for file system operations, making it straightforward to implement the required directory management and file organization features in "LibraGo".

Creating Directories Based on Authors

To organize book files by author, "LibraGo" can create a directory for each author and move their books into the respective directories.

```go
import (
    "os"
    "path/filepath"
)

func OrganizeBooksByAuthor(libraryPath string, books []Book) error {
    for _, book := range books {
        authorDir := filepath.Join(libraryPath, sanitizeFileName(book.Author))
        if err := os.MkdirAll(authorDir, 0755); err != nil {
            return err
        }

        originalPath := filepath.Join(libraryPath, book.FileName)
        newPath := filepath.Join(authorDir, book.FileName)
        if err := os.Rename(originalPath, newPath); err != nil {
            return err
        }
    }
    return nil
}

func sanitizeFileName(name string) string {
    // Implement filename sanitization to remove/replace invalid characters
    // This is platform-dependent and left as an exercise
```

return name

}

Cleaning Up Empty Directories

After organizing files, there might be empty directories left behind. Given below is how to clean those up:

```
func CleanupEmptyDirectories(rootDir string) error {

return filepath.Walk(rootDir, func(path string, info os.FileInfo, err error) error {

if err != nil {

return err

}

if info.IsDir() {

entries, err := os.ReadDir(path)

if err != nil {

return err

}

if len(entries) == 0 && path != rootDir {

if err := os.Remove(path); err != nil {

return err

}

}

}
```

```
    return nil
  })
}
```

Incorporating these directory management and file system operations into "LibraGo" helps users maintain a well-organized digital library.

```
func main() {
    libraryPath := "/path/to/digital/library"
    // Assuming books is populated with the user's digital book collection
    if err := OrganizeBooksByAuthor(libraryPath, books); err != nil {
        fmt.Printf("Failed to organize books by author: %s\n", err)
    }
    if err := CleanupEmptyDirectories(libraryPath); err != nil {
        fmt.Printf("Failed to clean up empty directories: %s\n", err)
    }
}
```

This function simplifies library administration, freeing up users to enjoy their collections rather than spend time administering them.

Recipe 8: Creating and Managing Temporary Files and Directories

Situation

The "LibraGo" application requires functionality to create temporary files and directories for intermediate processing tasks. These temporary resources should be easily identifiable, accessible during their brief lifecycle, and reliably cleaned up afterward to avoid clutter and waste of storage space. The challenge is to manage these resources efficiently, ensuring they are created, used, and deleted without manual intervention.

Practical Solution

Go's **io/ioutil** and **os** packages offer convenient functions for managing temporary files and directories. Using these, "LibraGo" can implement robust mechanisms for temporary resource management.

Creating a Temporary File

Temporary files can be created for storing intermediate data, such as processed book details before finalizing an import operation.

```go
import (

"io/ioutil"

"os"

)

func CreateTempFile(prefix string) (*os.File, error) {

tempFile, err := ioutil.TempFile("", prefix)

if err != nil {

return nil, err

}

// TempFile creates the file with os.O_RDWR|os.O_CREATE|os.O_EXCL mode

return tempFile, nil

}
```

Creating a Temporary Directory

Similarly, temporary directories are useful for operations that require organizing multiple files or isolating processing tasks.

```go
func CreateTempDir(prefix string) (string, error) {

    tempDir, err := ioutil.TempDir("", prefix)

    if err != nil {

    return "", err

    }

    return tempDir, nil

}
```

Using and Cleaning Up Temporary Resources

After using temporary files or directories, "LibraGo" ensures they are removed to free up space. This cleanup process is crucial and should be handled gracefully, even in the face of errors during processing.

```go
func ProcessAndCleanupTempFile(tempFile *os.File) {

    // Example processing on tempFile

    // ...

    // Cleanup

    defer os.Remove(tempFile.Name())

}

func ProcessAndCleanupTempDir(tempDir string) {

    // Example processing using tempDir

    // ...

    // Cleanup

    defer os.RemoveAll(tempDir)
```

}

Integrating temporary file and directory management into "LibraGo" enhances its capability to handle intermediate processing tasks efficiently.

```go
func main() {

    tempFile, err := CreateTempFile("librago")

    if err != nil {

        fmt.Printf("Failed to create a temporary file: %s\n", err)

        return

    }

    ProcessAndCleanupTempFile(tempFile)

    tempDir, err := CreateTempDir("librago")

    if err != nil {

        fmt.Printf("Failed to create a temporary directory: %s\n", err)

        return

    }

    ProcessAndCleanupTempDir(tempDir)

}
```

"LibraGo" can handle intermediate data processing jobs quickly by using Go's support for managing temporary files and directories. That way, managing digital libraries will always be a breeze, and the app will stay clean and efficient.

Summary

This chapter provided us with a full toolkit for handling and manipulating files and data in the

"LibraGo" application. Starting with the fundamentals of reading and writing files, the chapter advanced to more complicated topics including managing JSON and XML data, which are critical for compatibility with other systems and services. We learnt how to efficiently persist book information as well as serialize and deserialize complicated data structures, allowing for easy data sharing and storage.

The research proceeded with the use of regular expressions to parse unstructured text input, demonstrating Go's adaptability in extracting and manipulating information from multiple sources. This capability is especially useful for importing book details from various formats. In addition, we investigated CSV and text data processing, allowing "LibraGo" to handle one of the most used data interchange formats with ease. The chapter also offered approaches for binary data management, which addressed the need to manage digital assets such as book cover images in addition to textual data, hence improving the application's usefulness.

Advanced file system operations and directory management were learned, as well as tips for properly organizing digital collections and keeping them clutter-free. The chapter concluded with the creation and maintenance of temporary files and directories, which provided strategies for managing intermediate data processing chores in a clean and efficient manner. Each recipe built on the previous one, resulting in a sophisticated set of functionalities that allow users to manage their digital libraries more easily and efficiently, exhibiting Go's powerful capabilities for file handling and data processing in real-world applications.

Chapter 4: Building and Managing Go APIs

Introduction

Jumping into the construction of web APIs—a crucial component for modern applications—this chapter intends to take our "LibraGo" trip to the next level. This chapter covers the fundamentals of developing scalable, efficient, and secure APIs in Go, catering to a wide range of requirements from basic data retrieval to real-time communication. Through a series of thorough recipes, you will learn how to build a foundational HTTP server, the backbone of web communication, and progress to implementing a full-fledged RESTful API that follows best practices for resource handling and client-server interaction.

The first step in API development is to build up a basic HTTP server, which introduces the essential techniques for managing online requests and responses. This fundamental understanding is critical as we progress to more sophisticated topics such as the design and development of RESTful APIs. These APIs are designed to be scalable and flexible, allowing for easy data transmission and manipulation. We will look at effective request processing tactics, including how to use middleware to intercept and change requests for logging, authentication, and input validation.

Authentication procedures are rigorously reviewed to ensure safe access to API endpoints, which is an important part of preserving resources and data integrity. The chapter also delves into real-time communication via WebSockets, allowing for dynamic interactions between the server and clients, which is critical for features that require fast updates. Furthermore, we learn the necessity of API versioning and documentation in guaranteeing maintainability and developer friendliness, as well as methodologies for rigorous testing and debugging of API endpoints to ensure reliability and resilience.

By the end of this chapter, you will be able to build, manage, and scale APIs with Go, transforming the "LibraGo" application into a powerful platform for library management, with capabilities ranging from basic CRUD operations to real-time data synchronization and secure access control, encompassing the entire spectrum of API development.

Recipe 1: Building a Basic HTTP Server

Situation

To make "LibraGo" accessible over the web, we need to establish an HTTP server that can listen for requests on a specified port. The server must be capable of handling basic web requests, serving as the infrastructure for more complex API functionalities that will be developed subsequently.

Practical Solution

Go's standard library provides the **net/http** package, offering a robust set of functionalities for building HTTP servers.

Following is how to start a basic HTTP server and define handlers for responding to web requests:

```go
package main

import (

"fmt"

"net/http"

)

// homePage serves as the handler for the root route.

func homePage(w http.ResponseWriter, r *http.Request) {

fmt.Fprintf(w, "Welcome to the LibraGo Library Management System")

}

// setupRoutes defines routes and associates them with handlers.

func setupRoutes() {

http.HandleFunc("/", homePage)

}

func main() {

setupRoutes()

fmt.Println("LibraGo server is running on port 8080...")

// ListenAndServe starts the HTTP server on port 8080.

if err := http.ListenAndServe(":8080", nil); err != nil {

fmt.Println("Failed to start server:", err)

}
```

}

In the above sample program, we define a simple handler function **homePage** that outputs a welcome message. This function is mapped to the root URL path ("/") using **http.HandleFunc**. The server is then started on port 8080 using **http.ListenAndServe**, which listens for HTTP requests and dispatches them to the appropriate handler functions.

This basic server setup is the initial step towards making "LibraGo" a fully-featured web application. As we progress through the chapter, we will expand upon this foundation, adding routes and handlers for various API functionalities such as adding, listing, and managing books in the library.

Recipe 2: Handling HTTP Requests and Responses Effectively

Situation

With the basic HTTP server in place, the next step is to efficiently manage incoming HTTP requests and produce appropriate responses. "LibraGo" needs to handle various types of requests, such as GET for retrieving book information and POST for adding new books to the library. The application must parse request data, handle errors gracefully, and structure responses in a consistent format.

Practical Solution

To enhance request handling, we introduce route-specific handlers and explore parsing request bodies and query parameters. Additionally, we will implement error handling and response formatting to ensure a smooth interaction between "LibraGo" and its clients.

Implementing Route-Specific Handlers

For better organization, define separate handlers for different actions. Given below is an example handler for adding a new book via a POST request:

```
func addBookHandler(w http.ResponseWriter, r *http.Request) {

 if r.Method != http.MethodPost {

 http.Error(w, "Method is not supported.", http.StatusMethodNotAllowed)
```

```go
    return
}

var newBook Book
err := json.NewDecoder(r.Body).Decode(&newBook)
if err != nil {
    http.Error(w, err.Error(), http.StatusBadRequest)
    return
}
// Add the new book to the library (logic to add book not shown)

w.Header().Set("Content-Type", "application/json")
w.WriteHeader(http.StatusCreated)
json.NewEncoder(w).Encode(newBook)
}
```

Parsing Query Parameters

For operations like listing books with filters, parse query parameters from the request URL:

```go
func listBooksHandler(w http.ResponseWriter, r *http.Request) {
    if r.Method != http.MethodGet {
        http.Error(w, "Method is not supported.", http.StatusMethodNotAllowed)
        return
    }
```

```
// Example: /books?author=John+Doe
author := r.URL.Query().Get("author")
// Logic to filter books by author (not shown)
w.Header().Set("Content-Type", "application/json")
json.NewEncoder(w).Encode(books) // Assume books is the filtered list
}
```

Setting up Routes

Map each handler to a specific route in your setup function:

```
func setupRoutes() {
 http.HandleFunc("/books/add", addBookHandler)
 http.HandleFunc("/books/list", listBooksHandler)
}
```

With these handlers in place, "LibraGo" can effectively manage different types of HTTP requests, parsing incoming data and responding appropriately. This setup ensures that users can interact with the library system through a web interface, adding new books and retrieving lists of books based on specific criteria.

Recipe 3: Developing RESTful APIs

Situation

We need to codify the server-client interface as "LibraGo" develops further. In order to build, read, update, and delete (CRUD) books from the library, the app needs a RESTful API. By offering consistent and transparent endpoints and making semantic use of HTTP methods, this API should adhere to REST standards.

Practical Solution

To develop a RESTful API for "LibraGo," we will define endpoints that correspond to specific actions on the book resources, using the appropriate HTTP methods (GET, POST, PUT, DELETE) to reflect the actions being performed.

Defining the Book Resource Endpoints

- Create a Book (POST /books): Adds a new book to the library.
- List Books (GET /books): Retrieves a list of all books or a subset based on query parameters.
- Get a Book (GET /books/{id}): Retrieves the details of a specific book by ID.
- Update a Book (PUT /books/{id}): Updates the details of an existing book.
- Delete a Book (DELETE /books/{id}): Removes a book from the library.

Implementing the Endpoints

Following is an implementation outline for the "Create a Book" and "List Books" endpoints:

```go
func createBookHandler(w http.ResponseWriter, r *http.Request) {

    if r.Method != "POST" {

        http.Error(w, "Only POST method is allowed", http.StatusMethodNotAllowed)

        return

    }

    var book Book

    if err := json.NewDecoder(r.Body).Decode(&book); err != nil {

        http.Error(w, err.Error(), http.StatusBadRequest)

        return

    }

    // Logic to add the book to the library (omitted for brevity)

    w.WriteHeader(http.StatusCreated)

    json.NewEncoder(w).Encode(book)
```

```go
}
func listBooksHandler(w http.ResponseWriter, r *http.Request) {
    if r.Method != "GET" {
        http.Error(w, "Only GET method is allowed", http.StatusMethodNotAllowed)
        return
    }
    // Logic to retrieve books from the library (omitted for brevity)
    w.WriteHeader(http.StatusOK)
    json.NewEncoder(w).Encode(books) // Assume books is the list of all books
}
```

Routing

Enhance the **setupRoutes** function to include the new endpoints, using a router or the **http.HandleFunc** for simplicity:

```go
func setupRoutes() {
    http.HandleFunc("/books", createBookHandler) // Handles both creation and listing
    // Additional routes for getting, updating, and deleting books
}
```

Now that these endpoints are in place, "LibraGo" users can utilize a RESTful interface to conduct CRUD operations on their book collection. By making "LibraGo" more interactive and user-friendly, this advancement marks a key milestone.

Recipe 4: Implementing Middleware for Request Processing

Situation

The importance of security measures, log maintenance, and endpoint-wide request validation increases as the complexity of "LibraGo" increases. There would be code repetition and inconsistencies if these capabilities were manually added to every handler. The task at hand is to put into place a middleware solution that streamlines the request processing pipeline by applying common functions to requests before they reach the endpoint handlers.

Practical Solution

Middleware in Go can be implemented as functions that take a **http.Handler** and return a new **http.Handler**. By wrapping the original handler, middleware can execute pre- and post-processing logic on the requests and responses.

Following is how to create and apply middleware in "LibraGo":

Defining a Middleware Function

We will implement a simple logging middleware as an example. This middleware logs the details of each request to the console.

```
func loggingMiddleware(next http.Handler) http.Handler {

    return http.HandlerFunc(func(w http.ResponseWriter, r *http.Request) {

    // Log the request

    fmt.Printf("Received request: %s %s\n", r.Method, r.RequestURI)

    // Call the next handler

    next.ServeHTTP(w, r)

    })

}
```

Applying Middleware to Handlers

Middleware can be applied to handlers using a function that wraps the handlers with the middleware. If using the default **http.ServeMux** router, you can apply middleware directly to routes when setting them up:

```go
func applyMiddleware(handler http.Handler, middleware ...func(http.Handler) http.Handler) http.Handler {
    for _, m := range middleware {
        handler = m(handler)
    }
    return handler
}

func setupRoutes() {
    http.Handle("/books", applyMiddleware(http.HandlerFunc(createBookHandler), loggingMiddleware))
    // Apply the same middleware pattern to other handlers
}
```

Building a Middleware Chain

For more complex scenarios, you might need to chain multiple middleware functions. This can be achieved by sequentially wrapping handlers with multiple middleware:

```go
func authenticationMiddleware(next http.Handler) http.Handler {
    return http.HandlerFunc(func(w http.ResponseWriter, r *http.Request) {
        // Authentication logic (omitted for brevity)
        // Proceed to the next handler if authentication succeeds
        next.ServeHTTP(w, r)
    })
}
```

```
// Example of chaining middleware with authentication and logging

http.Handle("/books", applyMiddleware(http.HandlerFunc(createBookHandler), authenticationMiddleware, loggingMiddleware))
```

The application's logging, authentication, and request validation capabilities are improved by incorporating middleware into "LibraGo," which also helps to keep the business logic in our handlers clean. This method encourages code reusability and follows the DRY (Don't Repeat Yourself) concept, which makes the API more secure and easier to maintain.

Recipe 5: Authentication Mechanisms in API Development

Situation

Endpoint security is also becoming more important as "LibraGo" becomes available online. To prevent unauthorized users from adding or removing books or accessing other sensitive endpoints, the app requires a strong authentication system. One of the biggest obstacles is developing an authentication method that doesn't negatively impact the user experience.

Practical Solution

A common and effective approach for API authentication is using JSON Web Tokens (JWT). JWTs provide a compact and self-contained way to securely transmit information between parties as a JSON object. This method enables stateless authentication, where the server does not need to keep a record of tokens.

Generating and Validating JWT Tokens

First, add a dependency to your Go project for handling JWT. One widely used package is **github.com/dgrijalva/jwt-go**. (Always check for the most current and secure library version or alternatives.)

```
go get github.com/dgrijalva/jwt-go
```

User Authentication Endpoint

Create an endpoint where users can authenticate by submitting their credentials. Upon successful authentication, the server generates and returns a JWT.

```go
import (
    "github.com/dgrijalva/jwt-go"
    "net/http"
    "time"
)

var jwtKey = []byte("your_secret_key") // Keep this key secure

func generateJWT() (string, error) {
    expirationTime := time.Now().Add(1 * time.Hour)
    claims := &jwt.StandardClaims{
        ExpiresAt: expirationTime.Unix(),
    }
    token := jwt.NewWithClaims(jwt.SigningMethodHS256, claims)
    tokenString, err := token.SignedString(jwtKey)
    return tokenString, err
}

func loginHandler(w http.ResponseWriter, r *http.Request) {
    // Validate user credentials (omitted for brevity)

    tokenString, err := generateJWT()
    if err != nil {
        http.Error(w, "Failed to generate token", http.StatusInternalServerError)
```

```
    return
}

// Return the JWT token to the client
w.Write([]byte(tokenString))
}
```

Middleware for JWT Validation

Implement middleware to validate the JWT on protected endpoints. This middleware checks for a valid token in the request headers.

```
func jwtMiddleware(next http.Handler) http.Handler {
    return http.HandlerFunc(func(w http.ResponseWriter, r *http.Request) {
        const bearerPrefix = "Bearer "
        authHeader := r.Header.Get("Authorization")
        if !strings.HasPrefix(authHeader, bearerPrefix) {
            http.Error(w, "Unauthorized", http.StatusUnauthorized)
            return
        }
        tokenString := authHeader[len(bearerPrefix):]
        claims := &jwt.StandardClaims{}
        token, err := jwt.ParseWithClaims(tokenString, claims, func(token *jwt.Token) (interface{}, error) {
            return jwtKey, nil
        })
```

```
if err != nil || !token.Valid {

http.Error(w, "Unauthorized", http.StatusUnauthorized)

return

}

next.ServeHTTP(w, r)

})

}
```

With JWT authentication in place, "LibraGo" now has a secure mechanism for user authentication. Endpoints that modify library data can be protected with the JWT middleware, ensuring that only authenticated requests are processed.

```
func setupRoutes() {

http.HandleFunc("/login", loginHandler)

http.Handle("/books/add", jwtMiddleware(http.HandlerFunc(addBookHandler)))

// Additional protected routes

}
```

The authentication technique improves the security of "LibraGo," protecting user data and making sure that only authorized users may make changes to the library. Making LibraGo's web API secure and dependable requires implementing JWT authentication.

Recipe 6: Real-Time Communication with WebSockets

Situation

Real-time interactions are a feature of the "LibraGo" application, which is designed to increase user engagement. Live updates and interactive communication aren't good fits for the request-response approach that traditional HTTP queries follow. The task at hand is to set up a persistent, full-duplex communication channel between the server and the client, so that they can exchange messages in real-time without having to send additional HTTP requests.

Practical Solution

WebSockets provide a solution for maintaining a continuous connection between the client and server, ideal for the real-time features envisioned for "LibraGo". To implement WebSockets in Go, we can use the **gorilla/websocket** package, a popular and robust library that simplifies working with WebSockets.

First, add the WebSocket library to your project:

go get github.com/gorilla/websocket

Setting up a WebSocket Endpoint

Create a WebSocket endpoint in "LibraGo" that clients can connect to. The below sample program demonstrates setting up a simple WebSocket server that echoes messages back to the client.

```
import (

 "net/http"

 "github.com/gorilla/websocket"

)

var upgrader = websocket.Upgrader{

 CheckOrigin: func(r *http.Request) bool {

  return true // Allow connections from any origin

 },

}

func echoHandler(w http.ResponseWriter, r *http.Request) {

 conn, err := upgrader.Upgrade(w, r, nil)
```

```go
    if err != nil {
        http.Error(w, "Could not open WebSocket connection", http.StatusBadRequest)
        return
    }
    defer conn.Close()
    for {
        messageType, message, err := conn.ReadMessage()
        if err != nil {
            // Handle error (e.g., client disconnected)
            break
        }
        // Echo the received message back to the client
        if err := conn.WriteMessage(messageType, message); err != nil {
            // Handle error
            break
        }
    }
}
```

Integrating WebSocket Communication

With the WebSocket server in place, "LibraGo" can now handle real-time communication. To integrate this into the application, define the route for the WebSocket endpoint:

```go
func setupRoutes() {

    http.HandleFunc("/ws/echo", echoHandler)

    // Other routes...

}
```

Client-Side Implementation

On the client side, establish a WebSocket connection to the server, send messages, and handle incoming messages. This can be done using JavaScript for web clients:

```javascript
const socket = new WebSocket('ws://localhost:8080/ws/echo');

socket.onopen = function(e) {

  console.log("Connection established");

  socket.send("Hello, server!");

};

socket.onmessage = function(event) {

  console.log(`Message from server: ${event.data}`);

};

socket.onclose = function(event) {

  console.log("Connection closed");

};

socket.onerror = function(error) {

  console.log(`WebSocket error: ${error.message}`);

};
```

The addition of WebSockets to "LibraGo" adds a new level of user involvement, enabling functions like real-time chats and live notifications. This update does double duty: it makes "LibraGo" more responsive and engaging, which enhances the user experience, and also opens up new avenues for community interaction.

Recipe 7: Versioning APIs and Creating Documentation for "LibraGo" Application

Situation

With ongoing development, "LibraGo" may introduce changes that could potentially break existing client implementations. To mitigate this, the application needs a strategy for versioning its API, allowing for incremental improvements without disrupting the service for current users. Additionally, as the API expands, maintaining up-to-date documentation becomes crucial for guiding you in utilizing the API effectively.

Practical Solution

Implementing API Versioning

There are several approaches to versioning an API, such as URI versioning, header versioning, and parameter versioning. For "LibraGo", we will adopt URI versioning for its simplicity and visibility. This involves including the version number in the API endpoint's path.

```
func setupRoutes() {

    http.HandleFunc("/api/v1/books", booksHandlerV1)

    http.HandleFunc("/api/v2/books", booksHandlerV2)

    // Define other versioned routes

}
```

In this scheme, **v1** and **v2** denote different versions of the API. Each version can have its own set of handlers that reflect the functionalities available at that stage of the API's development.

Creating API Documentation

Clear, comprehensive documentation is vital for any API. Tools like Swagger (OpenAPI) or API

Blueprint can automate the creation of documentation and provide interactive interfaces for testing API endpoints.

To document the "LibraGo" API, you could use Swagger by defining your API structure in a YAML or JSON file, which Swagger uses to generate human readable documentation automatically.

swagger: '2.0'

info:

 title: LibraGo API

 version: 1.0.0

paths:

 /books:

 get:

 summary: Lists all books in the library.

 responses:

 200:

 description: A list of books.

 schema:

 type: array

 items:

 $ref: '#/definitions/Book'

definitions:

 Book:

 type: object

```
    properties:
      title:
        type: string
      author:
        type: string
      pages:
        type: integer
```

Now that versioning is a part of the "LibraGo" API, programmers can choose the version that best suits their needs. This method promotes a stable and extensible API ecosystem while also improving the developer experience through thorough documentation.

Recipe 8: Testing and Debugging API Endpoints

Situation

There is a higher chance of errors and slowdowns as "LibraGo" grows to incorporate more API endpoints for digital library management. A methodical strategy for testing and troubleshooting these endpoints is necessary to reduce these risks. Making tests that account for all possible outcomes—successes, failures, edge cases, and performance benchmarks—is a significant challenge.

Practical Solution

Go offers powerful tools and libraries for testing and debugging, including the built-in **testing** package for unit and integration tests, and third-party tools like Postman for manual testing and debugging of API endpoints.

Unit Testing API Handlers

Unit tests in Go are written in **_test.go** files using the **testing** package. Given below is an example of testing an API handler:

```go
package main

import (
    "bytes"
    "net/http"
    "net/http/httptest"
    "testing"
)

func TestAddBookHandler(t *testing.T) {
    requestBody := []byte(`{"title":"Test Book","author":"Jane Doe","pages":123}`)
    req, err := http.NewRequest("POST", "/api/v1/books", bytes.NewBuffer(requestBody))
    if err != nil {
        t.Fatal(err)
    }
    rr := httptest.NewRecorder()
    handler := http.HandlerFunc(addBookHandler)
    handler.ServeHTTP(rr, req)
    if status := rr.Code; status != http.StatusCreated {
        t.Errorf("handler returned wrong status code: got %v want %v", status, http.StatusCreated)
    }
    // Additional assertions for response body, etc.
}
```

}

Performance Testing

Performance testing can be conducted using benchmark tests in Go or using tools like Apache JMeter. Benchmark tests in Go are written similarly to unit tests but use the **b *testing.B** parameter to measure performance:

```go
func BenchmarkListBooks(b *testing.B) {

for i := 0; i < b.N; i++ {

// Call listBooksHandler or another API handler to test performance

}

}
```

Debugging tools and a thorough suite of tests allow the "LibraGo" team to guarantee that their API endpoints work properly in all scenarios and keep performance good even when the application grows. In order to provide users with a dependable and effective service, it is essential to employ this thorough testing and debugging technique.

Summary

This chapter provided a thorough overview of how to use Go to build secure, scalable, and reliable web APIs. Beginning with the fundamentals of configuring a basic HTTP server, the chapter progressed to the complexities of handling HTTP requests and responses, creating the framework for the development of a REST API. This process highlighted the necessity of following REST principles, such as employing HTTP methods semantically and organizing endpoints to match resource operations, resulting in a clean and intuitive API design.

The investigation looked into more advanced areas of API development, such as the use of middleware to expedite request processing and the integration of authentication techniques, including JWT, to secure API endpoints. The voyage through real-time communication highlighted the use of WebSockets, which enhanced "LibraGo" with dynamic, interactive features. Furthermore, the topic on versioning and documentation underlined the need of maintaining backward compatibility and providing clear, accessible API documentation, which are critical for encouraging developer engagement and ensuring the API's lifespan. Testing and debugging methodologies concluded the chapter, providing you with the tools you need to ensure your APIs are stable, performant, and bug-free.

This chapter improved the "LibraGo" program by providing practical recipes and real-world examples, as well as significant insights into web API development best practices. By embracing these techniques, you can create APIs that not only fulfill current demands but are also ready for future growth, accelerating the creation of powerful and user-friendly online services.

Chapter 5: Implementing RPC and gRPC Services in Go

Introduction

A high-performance, open source universal RPC framework created by Google, gRPC, is the focus of this chapter as we integrate Remote Procedure Call (RPC). This chapter attempts to demonstrate the possibilities of gRPC in Go, which enables efficient, type-safe, and scalable communication between microservices or client-server components of "LibraGo". Through a series of focused recipes, we will study the entire gRPC ecosystem, from the fundamentals of defining protocol buffers (protobufs) to the complexities of securing, monitoring, and logging in gRPC services.

We begin with "Defining Protobufs and Service Contracts," which establishes the foundation for our gRPC services by describing structured data and service methods in a language-neutral style. This initial phase establishes unambiguous, robust service contracts, allowing for seamless interaction between different portions of the "LibraGo" system, regardless of the underlying language or platform. Moving on to "Building Robust gRPC Servers in Go" and "Crafting a gRPC Client," we look at the practical aspects of configuring gRPC servers and clients in Go, demonstrating how to bring the established service contracts to life through code.

The next recipes cover "Error Handling in gRPC Services," which covers ways for gracefully managing mistakes within the gRPC framework, and "Implementing Streaming Data with gRPC," which looks at both server-streaming and client-streaming patterns to efficiently handle real-time data flows. "Ensuring gRPC Connection Security" emphasizes the need of securing communication routes, including SSL/TLS encryption to protect data in transit. Finally, "Monitoring and Logging in gRPC Services" teach the critical techniques for maintaining observability and accountability in distributed systems, guaranteeing that "LibraGo" remains stable and maintainable as it grows.

At the chapter's conclusion, you will have the necessary information to include gRPC into your own Go applications, improving the "LibraGo" app's design with scalable, secure, and efficient communication features.

Recipe 1: Defining Protobufs and Service Contracts

Situation

To facilitate communication between the "LibraGo" application's services or between clients and servers, there is a need for a robust, platform-independent method of defining data structures and service interfaces. This method must support strong type-checking, versioning, and be performant for network communication.

Practical Solution

RPC and gRPC Explained

RPC is a protocol that allows a program to execute a procedure (function) in another address space (commonly on another computer on a shared network), making it appear like a local procedure call, without the programmer explicitly coding the details for the remote interaction. gRPC, a modern, high-performance framework that extends RPC, leverages HTTP/2 for transport, Protocol Buffers (protobuf) as the interface description language, and provides features like authentication, load balancing, and more.

Defining Protobufs

Protocol Buffers (protobuf) are Google's language-neutral, platform-neutral, extensible mechanism for serializing structured data, similar to XML or JSON but more efficient and simpler. You define how you want your data to be structured once, then use special generated source code to easily write and read your structured data to and from different data streams and using various languages.

Given below is how you might define a protobuf for a Book service in "LibraGo":

- Install Protocol Buffer Compiler: First, ensure you have the Protocol Buffer compiler installed (**protoc**) to compile **.proto** files into Go code.
- Define the Book Service Protobuf: Create a **book.proto** file in your project:

syntax = "proto3";

package librago;

// The book service definition.

service BookService {

  // Sends a book detail request

  rpc GetBook (BookRequest) returns (BookResponse) {}

  // Streams book updates

  rpc WatchBooks (WatchRequest) returns (stream BookResponse) {}

}

// The request message containing the user's ID.

```
message BookRequest {
  string id = 1;
}
// The response message containing the book's details.
message BookResponse {
  string id = 1;
  string title = 2;
  string author = 3;
  int32 pages = 4;
}
// The request message for watching book updates.
message WatchRequest {}
```

- Generate Go Code: Use the **protoc** compiler to generate Go code from your **.proto** file:

```
protoc --go_out=. --go_opt=paths=source_relative \
--go-grpc_out=. --go-grpc_opt=paths=source_relative \
book.proto
```

This generates Go files containing code for your defined messages and service interface, which you can then use in your application to implement and consume the gRPC service.

With the protobuf definitions and generated Go code, you are set to implement the "BookService" in "LibraGo". This process involves writing the server-side logic to handle the defined RPC calls and developing clients that consume the service, leveraging gRPC for efficient, type-safe communication across the application's components.

Recipe 2: Building Robust gRPC Servers

Situation

With the service contracts defined, "LibraGo" needs a server implementation to handle the specified RPC calls. The challenge lies in building a server that not only adheres to the defined protobuf contracts but also ensures performance, reliability, and scalability.

Practical Solution

To implement a gRPC server in Go, follow these steps, building upon the protobuf definitions and generated code from the previous recipe.

Install gRPC for Go

If not already done, ensure you have the gRPC library for Go installed:

```
go get google.golang.org/grpc
```

Implement the Server Interface

Based on the **book.proto** service definition, implement the server interface in Go. This involves creating functions for each RPC call defined in your protobuf file.

```go
package main

import (

 "context"

 "fmt"

 "log"

 "net"

 "google.golang.org/grpc"

 pb "path/to/your/protobuf/package" // Import path for the generated protobuf package

)
```

```go
// server is used to implement librago.BookService.
type server struct {
    pb.UnimplementedBookServiceServer
}

// GetBook implements librago.BookService.GetBook
func (s *server) GetBook(ctx context.Context, in *pb.BookRequest) (*pb.BookResponse, error) {
    // Implement logic to retrieve a book by ID
    return &pb.BookResponse{Id: in.GetId(), Title: "Example Title", Author: "Author Name", Pages: 123}, nil
}

// WatchBooks implements librago.BookService.WatchBooks
func (s *server) WatchBooks(req *pb.WatchRequest, srv pb.BookService_WatchBooksServer) error {
    // Implement logic to stream book updates
    return nil
}

func main() {
    lis, err := net.Listen("tcp", ":50051")
    if err != nil {
        log.Fatalf("failed to listen: %v", err)
    }
```

```
s := grpc.NewServer()

pb.RegisterBookServiceServer(s, &server{})

log.Printf("server listening at %v", lis.Addr())

if err := s.Serve(lis); err != nil {

log.Fatalf("failed to serve: %v", err)

}

}
```

Running the Server

Execute your server application. It will start listening for gRPC requests on the specified port (e.g., 50051). Ensure your firewall and network settings allow for incoming connections on this port if the server is to be accessible externally.

With the gRPC server implemented and running, "LibraGo" is now capable of handling RPC calls as defined in the service contract. This server acts as a central point for processing book-related operations, such as retrieving book details or streaming updates to clients in real-time.

Recipe 3: Crafting a gRPC Client

Situation

To fully utilize the "LibraGo" gRPC server's capabilities, there is a need for a client that can make requests to the server, such as fetching book details or subscribing to book updates. The challenge is to implement a client that is not only functional but also integrates seamlessly with the server, ensuring smooth communication between the two.

Practical Solution

Building a gRPC client in Go involves using the same protobuf definitions as the server. This ensures both the client and server share the same understanding of the data structures and service methods.

Initialize a gRPC Client Connection

Start by establishing a connection to the gRPC server using the **grpc.Dial** function. This connection is used to create a client stub that facilitates calling the server's methods.

```go
package main

import (
    "context"
    "log"
    "time"
    "google.golang.org/grpc"
    pb "path/to/your/protobuf/package" // Use the correct import path
)

func main() {
    // Set up a connection to the server.
    conn, err := grpc.Dial("localhost:50051", grpc.WithInsecure(), grpc.WithBlock())
    if err != nil {
        log.Fatalf("did not connect: %v", err)
    }
    defer conn.Close()
    c := pb.NewBookServiceClient(conn)
    // Contact the server and print out its response.
    ctx, cancel := context.WithTimeout(context.Background(), time.Second)
    defer cancel()
    r, err := c.GetBook(ctx, &pb.BookRequest{Id: "1"})
```

```
if err != nil {
log.Fatalf("could not get book: %v", err)
}
log.Printf("Book: %s", r.GetTitle())
}
```

Making Requests to the Server

Use the client stub (**c** in the example) to make RPC calls to the server. The above example demonstrates fetching a book by its ID using the **GetBook** method defined in the service contract. The client uses context to manage timeouts and cancelation signals.

Recipe 4: Handling Errors in gRPC Services

Situation

It is not sufficient to just terminate a gRPC service operation when it fails or encounters an issue. There has to be a system in place for handling problems in the "LibraGo" app that can classify them, give customers useful feedback, and implement retry logic as necessary. Developing a consistent method for managing errors that works in tandem with the gRPC architecture is the real obstacle.

Practical Solution

gRPC uses a rich set of error codes to convey various error conditions from the server to the client. Leveraging these error codes along with custom error metadata allows for precise error handling and communication.

Standard gRPC Error Codes

Utilize gRPC's predefined error codes to represent different types of errors, such as **NotFound**, **InvalidArgument**, **PermissionDenied**, etc. This helps clients understand the nature of the error without needing to parse error messages.

Returning Standard gRPC Errors

In Go, use the **status** package to return an error with a specific gRPC error code:

```go
import (
    "context"
    "google.golang.org/grpc/codes"
    "google.golang.org/grpc/status"
    pb "path/to/your/protobuf/package"
)

func (s *server) GetBook(ctx context.Context, in *pb.BookRequest) (*pb.BookResponse, error) {
    // Example error condition: book not found
    if bookNotFound {
        return nil, status.Errorf(codes.NotFound, "book with ID %s not found", in.GetId())
    }
    // Normal operation
    return &pb.BookResponse{/* ... */}, nil
}
```

Custom Error Metadata

For more detailed error information, attach custom metadata to the error response using trailers. This can include additional details about the error or corrective actions.

```go
md := metadata.Pairs("error-details", "Additional information about the error")
st, _ := status.New(codes.Internal, "internal error").WithDetails(md)
err := st.Err()
```

Client-Side Error Handling

On the client side, interpret the error codes and metadata to implement appropriate error handling logic:

```
resp, err := c.GetBook(ctx, &pb.BookRequest{Id: "non-existent-id"})

if err != nil {

st, ok := status.FromError(err)

if ok {

// Use st.Code() to handle different error codes

fmt.Printf("Error code: %v, message: %s\n", st.Code(), st.Message())

// Handle custom metadata if present

if md, ok := metadata.FromIncomingContext(ctx); ok {

fmt.Println(md["error-details"])

}

} else {

// Non-gRPC error handling

}

}
```

The application's communication patterns are made more resilient and reliable, and the user experience is improved by receiving clear and actionable error information. In order to create an application architecture that is both resilient and easy to maintain, this method makes sure that clients and servers can handle faults well.

Recipe 5: Implementing Streaming Data with gRPC

Situation

Users of "LibraGo" will always have access to the most recent data without having to refresh or poll the server manually because of the system's ability to transmit updates to clients in real-time. The difficulty lies in developing a dependable streaming system that can manage constant data transfers between the client and server.

Practical Solution

gRPC supports four types of streaming: server streaming, client streaming, bidirectional streaming, and no streaming (simple RPC). For "LibraGo", we will focus on server streaming to push book updates to clients, and bidirectional streaming for a more interactive communication pattern.

Server Streaming RPC

Server streaming RPCs allow the server to send multiple messages to the client after receiving a client's request. This is suitable for scenarios like sending live updates to clients.

- Define the Server Streaming Service in Protobuf: Update your **book.proto** file to define a server streaming RPC method:

```
service BookService {

rpc ListBookUpdates(BookUpdatesRequest) returns (stream Book) {}

}
```

- Implement the Server Streaming Method: On the server, implement the **ListBookUpdates** method to stream book updates to the client.

```
func (s *server) ListBookUpdates(req *pb.BookUpdatesRequest, stream pb.BookService_ListBookUpdatesServer) error {

// Example: stream updates for a book

for _, book := range books { // Assume books is a slice of Book objects

if err := stream.Send(&book); err != nil {

return err
```

}

}

return nil

}

Bidirectional Streaming RPC

Bidirectional streaming allows both the client and server to send a stream of messages independently, enabling interactive communication.

- Define the Bidirectional Streaming Service in Protobuf:

service BookService {

rpc Chat(stream ChatMessage) returns (stream ChatMessage) {}

}

- Implement the Bidirectional Streaming Method: Implement a method where both the server and client can send messages back and forth.

func (s *server) Chat(stream pb.BookService_ChatServer) error {

for {

in, err := stream.Recv()

if err == io.EOF {

return nil

}

if err != nil {

return err

}

```
// Process incoming message and respond

responseMessage := processMessage(in)

if err := stream.Send(responseMessage); err != nil {
    return err
}
    }
}
```

With streaming implemented in "LibraGo", the application can now offer live updates and interactive features, significantly enhancing user engagement and the overall user experience.

Recipe 6: Ensuring gRPC Connection Security

Situation

Even though gRPC allows for versatile and efficient communication between the "LibraGo" app's parts, data transmitted over the network can be vulnerable to eavesdropping, manipulation, or man-in-the-middle attacks if not secured properly. Making sure gRPC connections are secure without making the system slower or more complicated is the real challenge. Let's see.

Practical Solution

TLS (Transport Layer Security) provides an encrypted communication channel between clients and servers, which is crucial for maintaining the confidentiality and integrity of the data being exchanged. Implementing TLS in gRPC involves generating SSL certificates and modifying both the client and server configurations to use these certificates.

Generate SSL Certificates

Use OpenSSL or any other SSL tool to generate a self-signed certificate for testing purposes. For production, consider acquiring certificates from a trusted CA (Certificate Authority).

```
openssl genrsa -out server.key 2048
```

openssl req -new -x509 -sha256 -key server.key -out server.crt -days 3650

Configure the gRPC Server for TLS

Modify the server initialization code to load the SSL certificates and start the server with TLS.

```go
import "google.golang.org/grpc/credentials"

func main() {

lis, err := net.Listen("tcp", ":50051")

if err != nil {

log.Fatalf("failed to listen: %v", err)

}

creds, err := credentials.NewServerTLSFromFile("server.crt", "server.key")

if err != nil {

log.Fatalf("Failed to generate credentials %v", err)

}

s := grpc.NewServer(grpc.Creds(creds))

pb.RegisterBookServiceServer(s, &server{})

//...

}
```

Configure the gRPC Client for TLS

The client also needs to be aware of the TLS configuration to securely connect to the server.

```go
creds, err := credentials.NewClientTLSFromFile("server.crt", "")

if err != nil {
```

```go
    log.Fatalf("Failed to create TLS credentials %v", err)
}

conn, err := grpc.Dial("localhost:50051", grpc.WithTransportCredentials(creds))
if err != nil {
    log.Fatalf("did not connect: %v", err)
}
defer conn.Close()
//...
```

TLS encrypts all gRPC communication in "LibraGo" to protect user data and interactions. Enhancing the entire security posture of the "LibraGo" application and building trust with users by protecting their data integrity and privacy is the goal of this strategy.

Recipe 7: Adding Logging to gRPC Services

Situation

With the addition of gRPC services, "LibraGo" gets more complicated, and it's clear that thorough logging is necessary. Data regarding gRPC calls, including as requests, responses, error messages, and execution times, as well as other relevant information, must be captured by the application's logging solution. The trick is to implement the logging in a manner that gives you the information you need while causing the application's performance as little disruption as possible.

Practical Solution

For this purpose, we will introduce Zap, a high-performance logging tool designed for Go applications. Zap provides a perfect balance between speed and ease of use, offering structured logging with a simple API and advanced features like levelled logging and structured contexts.

Install Zap Logger

Begin by adding Zap to your project dependencies:

```
go get -u go.uber.org/zap
```

Setting up Zap Logger

Initialize Zap in your application to start logging gRPC requests and responses.

```go
import "go.uber.org/zap"

var logger *zap.Logger

func init() {
  // For production, use zap.NewProduction() for a sensible default
  // configuration. Here, we're using a development config for
  // rich, human-readable logs.
  logger, _ = zap.NewDevelopment()
}
```

Integrating Logging with gRPC Interceptors

Utilize gRPC interceptors to automatically log details about each gRPC call. Interceptors are special functions that gRPC executes for every incoming or outgoing call, providing a convenient hook for logging.

```go
import (
  "context"
  "google.golang.org/grpc"
  "google.golang.org/grpc/status"
)

// UnaryServerInterceptor returns a new unary server interceptors that adds zap log.
func UnaryServerInterceptor(logger *zap.Logger) grpc.UnaryServerInterceptor {
```

```go
return func(
    ctx context.Context,
    req interface{},
    info *grpc.UnaryServerInfo,
    handler grpc.UnaryHandler,
) (resp interface{}, err error) {
    // Log request
    logger.Info("gRPC request", zap.String("method", info.FullMethod), zap.Any("request", req))
    // Handle request
    resp, err = handler(ctx, req)
    // Log response
    st, _ := status.FromError(err)
    logger.Info("gRPC response",
        zap.String("method", info.FullMethod),
        zap.Any("response", resp),
        zap.String("status", st.Code().String()))
    return resp, err
}
}
```

Applying the Interceptor to the gRPC Server

When initializing your gRPC server, add the interceptor to capture and log all incoming requests.

```go
func main() {
    lis, err := net.Listen("tcp", ":50051")
    if err != nil {
        logger.Fatal("failed to listen", zap.Error(err))
    }
    s := grpc.NewServer(
        grpc.UnaryInterceptor(UnaryServerInterceptor(logger)),
    )
    // Register services and start server
}
```

With Zap logger integrated into "LibraGo" through gRPC interceptors, every aspect of the gRPC communication is logged, providing valuable insights into the system's behavior.

Summary

This chapter has taken us on a fascinating tour of contemporary service communication strategies. Beginning with the fundamental task of creating protobufs and service contracts, the chapter lay the foundations for developing clear, robust interfaces for gRPC services. This first stage was critical to ensuring that both the client and server components of "LibraGo" could communicate seamlessly, with a shared understanding of the data structures and actions involved. Building on this, the development of a powerful gRPC server and client demonstrated the practical features of implementing these service contracts, allowing for real-time, bidirectional communication that is both efficient and type-safe.

The chapter delves deeper into the complexities of gRPC, covering advanced subjects including error handling, streaming data, connection security, and adding logging to gRPC services. Through these recipes, "LibraGo" was augmented with advanced error management strategies, utilizing gRPC's extensive collection of error codes to properly express diverse fault scenarios. The addition of streaming data created new opportunities for real-time interactions within

"LibraGo", improving the user experience with live updates and interactive communication channels. Securing these connections with TLS/SSL encryption guaranteed that all conversations were confidential and tamper-proof, which is crucial for the application's trust and integrity. Finally, combining structured logging with Zap created a powerful monitoring and debugging tool, improving the "LibraGo" application's observability and maintainability.

As a whole, this chapter has done wonders for "LibraGo"'s technical capabilities and shed light on how to build gRPC services in Go through the best practices. These insights are critical for any developer trying to create scalable, secure, and efficient distributed systems, demonstrating the power and flexibility of gRPC in modern application development.

Chapter 6: Web Services and Automation Using Go

Introduction

The purpose of this chapter is to increase the functionality of the "LibraGo" app by improving the web interface and automating several processes to make the app more efficient and easier to use. This chapter digs into the practical features of web development and task automation using Go, demonstrating its versatility and power in managing web services and scripting.

We begin by investigating "Implementing Templating and Static Assets," in which we learn how to generate dynamic web pages using Go's templating engine while also managing static assets such as CSS, JavaScript, and pictures to enhance the "LibraGo" online interface. This lays the groundwork for creating more engaging and visually appealing online applications. Following that, "Building and Consuming Diverse Web Services" covers approaches for serving and consuming RESTful services and other web APIs, with a focus on how Go may be used to interact with a variety of web services seamlessly.

The chapter then moves on to "Effective Session Management in Web Apps," which is critical for retaining state and user data across the web application while also providing a safe and personalized user experience. "Automating Routine Tasks" and "Scheduling Tasks with Cron Jobs" focus on backend efficiencies, demonstrating how to automate repetitive tasks like data backups, report generation, and periodic data synchronization, all of which are required to keep the "LibraGo" application's data integrity and freshness.

Further investigation of "Integration with External APIs" demonstrates Go's ability to extend the functionality of the "LibraGo" application by leveraging third-party services such as payment gateways, social media feeds, or other data providers, hence increasing the application's feature set. Finally, "Creating Command-Line Tools" teach the creation of utility tools for administrative chores, which provide a powerful means to interface with the application's backend services directly from the command prompt.

Recipe 1: Implementing Templating and Static Assets

Situation

It is necessary to display information in a more interesting and structured way as "LibraGo" expands. When it comes to showing dynamic content, like library data that is individual to each user, static HTML pages just don't cut it. In addition, it is not easy to efficiently manage pictures, JavaScript, and CSS while keeping the application fluid and speedy.

Practical Solution

Templating and Static Assets

Templating in web development is a method to dynamically generate HTML pages by combining static templates with dynamic data. Templates define the structure of a webpage, with placeholders for data that gets filled in at runtime, allowing for content customization based on user interactions or other criteria.

Static Assets refer to files served directly by the web server without modification, typically including CSS for styling, JavaScript for functionality, and images or multimedia content. Efficient management and delivery of these assets are key to a fast and smooth user experience.

Implementing Templating with Go's **html/template**

Go's standard library includes powerful tools for templating, notably the **html/template** package, which allows for secure rendering of HTML content.

First, create an HTML file (**template.html**) defining the structure of your page with placeholders for dynamic data.

```html
<!DOCTYPE html>
<html>
<head>
 <title>{{.Title}}</title>
</head>
<body>
 <h1>{{.Heading}}</h1>
 <p>{{.Content}}</p>
</body>
</html>
```

In your Go server code, use the **html/template** package to parse the template file and inject dynamic data.

```go
import (
```

```go
    "html/template"
    "net/http"
)
func handler(w http.ResponseWriter, r *http.Request) {
    tmpl := template.Must(template.ParseFiles("template.html"))
    data := struct {
        Title   string
        Heading string
        Content string
    }{
        Title:   "LibraGo Library",
        Heading: "Welcome to LibraGo",
        Content: "Your personal library management system.",
    }
    tmpl.Execute(w, data)
}
```

Use Go's built-in file server to efficiently serve static assets from a designated directory.

```go
func main() {
    fs := http.FileServer(http.Dir("static"))
    http.Handle("/static/", http.StripPrefix("/static/", fs))
    http.HandleFunc("/", handler)
```

```go
    http.ListenAndServe(":8080", nil)
}
```

Place your CSS, JavaScript, and image files in a **static** directory within your project. The **http.FileServer** handler will serve these files under the **/static/** path.

The "LibraGo" program is able to provide a dynamic, physically attractive, and functionally strong user experience by combining templating with static asset management. This method improves the user experience and streamlines information and interactivity.

Recipe 2: Building and Consuming Web Services

Situation

The "LibraGo" app can be made more flexible and extend its capabilities by consuming other people's services and by offering its own features as web services. Services like this include accessing the "LibraGo" catalog via API or retrieving book details from other APIs. Creating web service connections, handling JSON or XML data, and managing network communication protocols are difficult.

Practical Solution

Go's **net/http** package provides a robust set of functionalities for creating web servers and handling HTTP requests, making it well-suited for building web services.

Create a RESTful API Endpoint

Define a handler function that responds to HTTP requests with JSON-formatted data, representing book details or other information provided by "LibraGo".

```go
import (

    "encoding/json"

    "net/http"

)
```

```go
type Book struct {
    ID string `json:"id"`
    Title string `json:"title"`
    Author string `json:"author"`
}
func bookHandler(w http.ResponseWriter, r *http.Request) {
    books := []Book{
        {ID: "1", Title: "Go Programming", Author: "John Doe"},
        // Add more books
    }
    w.Header().Set("Content-Type", "application/json")
    json.NewEncoder(w).Encode(books)
}
```

Consuming Web Services in Go

To consume external web services, use the **net/http** package to make HTTP requests and decode the responses.

Create a function to fetch data from an external API, parsing the JSON response into a Go struct.

```go
import (
    "encoding/json"
    "io/ioutil"
    "log"
    "net/http"
```

```go
)

func fetchBooks(url string) ([]Book, error) {

    resp, err := http.Get(url)

    if err != nil {

    return nil, err

    }

    defer resp.Body.Close()

    body, err := ioutil.ReadAll(resp.Body)

    if err != nil {

    return nil, err

    }

    var books []Book

    err = json.Unmarshal(body, &books)

    if err != nil {

    return nil, err

    }

    return books, nil

}
```

Handling JSON Data

Both when serving and consuming web services, handling JSON data is a common task. Use Go's **encoding/json** package to serialize structs to JSON when serving responses and to deserialize JSON responses into structs when consuming services.

These examples show the basic processes of expanding "LibraGo" to connect to the web, using Go's robust standard library to create and use web services. With its API endpoints, "LibraGo" can connect to more services and apps, and with the help of other APIs, it can access data and features from all over the web, enhancing its functionality.

Recipe 3: Effective Session Management in Web Apps

Situation

The fundamental design of web apps is that they do not retain user data between queries; this quality is known as statelessness. Session state maintenance is essential for many apps that need to keep tabs on user actions and preferences while they're on the site. In order to prevent unwanted access while still offering a smooth user experience, session management must strike a balance between usability, performance, and security.

Practical Solution

Session management in Go web applications can be handled through various methods, including cookies, token-based sessions, and third-party session management libraries.

Managing Sessions with Cookies

Cookies are small pieces of data stored in the user's browser and sent with each request to the server. They can be used to store session identifiers, linking the user to their session data stored server-side.

```go
import (

    "net/http"

    "time"

)

func setSessionCookie(w http.ResponseWriter, sessionID string) {

    // Set a cookie that expires in 1 hour

    http.SetCookie(w, &http.Cookie{
```

```
    Name: "session_token",
    Value: sessionID,
    Expires: time.Now().Add(1 * time.Hour),
})
}
```

Token-Based Session Management

Token-based sessions, such as JWT (JSON Web Tokens), provide a way to maintain session state by passing a secure token back and forth between the client and server. This token contains encoded session data that can be verified and decoded by the server on each request.

```
import (
    "github.com/dgrijalva/jwt-go"
    "time"
)

func createSessionToken(secretKey string) (string, error) {
    // Create a new token object, specifying signing method and claims
    token := jwt.NewWithClaims(jwt.SigningMethodHS256, jwt.MapClaims{
        "user_id": "123456",
        "exp": time.Now().Add(time.Hour * 72).Unix(),
    })
    // Sign and get the complete encoded token as a string
    tokenString, err := token.SignedString([]byte(secretKey))
    return tokenString, err
```

}

Session Storage

Depending on the application's scale and requirements, session data can be stored in various backends, from in-memory stores like **sync.Map** or external databases and caching solutions like Redis. The choice of storage affects the application's performance, scalability, and reliability.

Security Considerations
- Ensure session identifiers are generated using secure, unpredictable values to prevent session hijacking.
- Implement HTTPS to encrypt cookies and tokens in transit, protecting them from eavesdropping and man-in-the-middle attacks.
- Consider setting cookie attributes like **HttpOnly** and **Secure** to further enhance security.

Recipe 4: Automating Routine Tasks

Situation

Tasks like database backups, report generation, and data synchronization are common in web applications and typically need to run at specific intervals or under specific situations. It is not only time-consuming but also error-prone to do these operations by hand. The problem is to find an automated solution that can reliably carry out these repetitive operations without requiring any human interaction.

Practical Solution

Go's support for concurrency with goroutines and channels provides a powerful mechanism for automating tasks. You can use these features to run background tasks, schedule jobs, or even perform operations in parallel to improve performance.

Creating a Simple Background Task Runner

Define a function that encapsulates the task you want to automate, and use a goroutine to run it in the background. This is particularly useful for tasks that need to run continuously or at regular intervals.

import (

"log"

```go
    "time"
)

func backupDatabase() {
    for {
        log.Println("Starting database backup...")
        // Logic for backing up the database
        time.Sleep(24 * time.Hour) // Example: Run once every 24 hours
    }
}

func main() {
    go backupDatabase()
    // The main function continues to run, and backupDatabase runs in the background
}
```

Scheduling Tasks

For more complex scheduling beyond simple intervals, consider using a third-party package like **robfig/cron** that supports cron expressions for defining more sophisticated scheduling patterns.

```go
import (
    "github.com/robfig/cron/v3"
    "log"
)

func performDataSync() {
```

```go
log.Println("Performing data synchronization...")
// Data synchronization logic here
}
func main() {
c := cron.New()
c.AddFunc("@daily", performDataSync) // Runs performDataSync once every day
c.Start()
// Keep the application running
select {}
}
```

Recipe 5: Scheduling Tasks with Cron Jobs

Cron jobs are tasks scheduled to run automatically at fixed times, dates, or intervals. In Go, the **robfig/cron** package is a popular choice for implementing cron job scheduling, providing a powerful and flexible way to manage task execution.

Setting up the Cron Package

First, ensure the **cron** package is included in your project:

```
go get github.com/robfig/cron/v3
```

Creating a Cron Job Scheduler

Instantiate a new cron scheduler and define jobs with specific schedules. Cron expressions offer fine-grained control over when the tasks are executed.

```go
import (
    "fmt"
```

```go
    "github.com/robfig/cron/v3"
    "time"
)

func main() {
    c := cron.New()
    // Run a task every hour
    c.AddFunc("@hourly", func() {
        fmt.Println("Running task -", time.Now().Format(time.RFC1123))
        // Task logic here
    })
    // Start the scheduler (non-blocking)
    c.Start()
    // Keep the application running
    select {}
}
```

Cron Expressions

Cron expressions are strings that represent a schedule in a cron format. For example, **"0 * * * *"** represents a task that runs at the top of every hour. The **robfig/cron** library supports standard cron expressions and predefined schedules like **@hourly**, **@daily**, and **@weekly**.

Error Handling and Job Inspection

When adding tasks, it's important to handle potential errors, especially if the cron expression might be dynamically specified. The **cron** package returns an error if the schedule expression is invalid. Additionally, each job can be assigned an ID, allowing for later inspection or removal.

```
entryID, err := c.AddFunc("@daily", func() { fmt.Println("Daily task") })
if err != nil {
 log.Fatalf("Error scheduling task: %v", err)
}
// Later, you might inspect or remove the job using entryID
```

Advanced Scheduling

The **cron** library allows for more sophisticated scheduling features, such as job chaining, named jobs, and time zones support, enabling precise control over task execution in complex scenarios.

Recipe 6: Integration with External APIs

API (Application Programming Interface) integration involves programmatically interacting with external services to retrieve data or perform operations outside your application's native capabilities. This could include sending emails through a third-party service, fetching book details from a public API, or processing payments.

Implementing External API Calls

Go's standard library provides robust tools for making HTTP requests, which is a common method for interacting with RESTful APIs.

Following is how you can integrate an external RESTful service into your application:

Set up HTTP Client

Create a reusable HTTP client. This allows for connection reuse and other optimizations.

```
import (
 "net/http"
 "time"
)
var httpClient = &http.Client{
```

```go
Timeout: time.Second * 10,
}
```

Making a GET Request

For retrieving data from an external API, send a GET request and parse the response.

```go
import (
"encoding/json"
"fmt"
"io/ioutil"
"log"
)
type BookDetails struct {
Title string `json:"title"`
Author string `json:"author"`
Pages int `json:"pages"`
}
func fetchBookDetails(apiURL string) (*BookDetails, error) {
resp, err := httpClient.Get(apiURL)
if err != nil {
return nil, err
}
defer resp.Body.Close()
```

```go
    body, err := ioutil.ReadAll(resp.Body)
    if err != nil {
        return nil, err
    }
    var book BookDetails
    if err := json.Unmarshal(body, &book); err != nil {
        return nil, err
    }
    return &book, nil
}
```

Handling POST Requests

To send data to an external service, use a POST request with an appropriate payload.

```go
import (
    "bytes"
    "net/http"
)

func createExternalResource(apiURL string, data []byte) error {
    req, err := http.NewRequest("POST", apiURL, bytes.NewBuffer(data))
    if err != nil {
        return err
    }
```

```
req.Header.Set("Content-Type", "application/json")

resp, err := httpClient.Do(req)

if err != nil {

return err

}

defer resp.Body.Close()

// Handle response (omitted for brevity)

return nil

}
```

Security and Authentication

When integrating with external APIs, consider security and authentication mechanisms. Many APIs require API keys or OAuth tokens for access. Ensure these credentials are securely stored and correctly included in your API requests. Be mindful of rate limits imposed by external services to avoid service disruption. Implement robust error handling to manage API failures gracefully, ensuring your application can respond to or recover from such situations.

Recipe 7: Creating Command-Line Tools

In order to build command-line tools, one must be able to interpret command-line arguments, run operations according to those arguments, and then display feedback on the console. The standard library and third-party packages in Go provide strong support for developing these tools, making it easy to design command-line interfaces (CLIs) that are both efficient and user-friendly.

Implementing a Basic CLI Tool in Go

Go's **flag** package is a simple yet powerful way to parse command-line arguments. It supports basic data types and allows for default values.

```
import (

"flag"
```

```go
    "fmt"
)
func main() {
    // Define flags
    name := flag.String("name", "World", "a name to say hello to")
    times := flag.Int("times", 1, "how many times to say hello")
    // Parse the flags
    flag.Parse()
    // Use the flag values
    for i := 0; i < *times; i++ {
        fmt.Printf("Hello, %s!\n", *name)
    }
}
```

Running this tool with **./tool -name=Go -times=3** would print "Hello, Go!" three times.

For more complex CLI tools that require subcommands and more sophisticated argument parsing, consider using a third-party package like **cobra** or **urfave/cli**. These packages offer enhanced functionality for building structured and intuitive command-line applications.

Using Cobra

Cobra is a popular library for creating powerful CLI applications. It supports subcommands, nested commands, flags, and auto-generated documentation.

go get -u github.com/spf13/cobra@latest

Cobra uses a command structure where each command can have its own flags and subcommands.

```go
import (
    "github.com/spf13/cobra"
    "fmt"
)

func main() {
    var rootCmd = &cobra.Command{
        Use: "greet",
        Short: "Greet command",
        Long: `A longer description of the greet command.`,
        Run: func(cmd *cobra.Command, args []string) {
            fmt.Println("Hello, Cobra CLI!")
        },
    }
    rootCmd.Execute()
}
```

You may build anything from basic utilities to complicated apps with several subcommands using Go's extensive support for command line development. This will improve your app's usability and automation possibilities.

Summary

In this chapter, we looked at ways to improve web applications by automating mundane tasks, integrating with external services seamlessly, and delivering content dynamically. This chapter lays the groundwork for creating a rich user experience by introducing methods to build responsive and interactive web pages, beginning with developing templating and managing static assets. Using Go's templating engine in conjunction with efficient handling of pictures, JavaScript, and CSS allows you to create dynamic, engaging, and performant online interfaces.

Additional research into creating and using web services highlights Go's capacity to communicate with numerous external APIs, allowing the program to expand its capabilities without starting from scratch. We go over several good session management techniques that can keep user context and information intact in HTTP communications, which are essentially stateless, so that users can have safe, tailored interactions. The chapter concludes by highlighting the significance of cron jobs for automating and scheduling mundane operations, demonstrating Go's ability to create strong background processes that improve application efficiency and stability. Applications can take advantage of third-party services and provide consumers with more features when they integrate with external APIs.

The last recipe, which involves making command-line tools, demonstrates how versatile Go is outside of web contexts; it allows you to create utilities that communicate directly with the application's backend, which simplifies administrative tasks and automates workflows. From automating data synchronization to safeguarding web interactions, this chapter showcases Go's strengths in creating modern web services and automation tools through its emphasis on practical solutions. This in-depth analysis does double duty: it teaches you how to use Go to improve web applications and it generates new ideas for tackling typical development problems.

Chapter 7: Building Microservices Architecture Using Go

Introduction

The focus of this chapter is on designing and implementing microservices using Go, taking use of its simplicity, concurrency, and performance advantages. This chapter intends to provide you with the skills and knowledge required to design, create, and manage microservices, resulting in scalable, manageable, and efficient distributed systems. The chapter teaches the challenges and best practices of constructing microservices from the ground up by dissecting various components of the architecture using practical recipes.

The adventure begins with "Designing and Implementing a Go Microservice," where we learn about the fundamentals of microservices architecture, with a focus on developing loosely connected services that encapsulate specific business functions. This recipe covers the fundamentals of building a Go microservice, such as setting service boundaries, data management strategies, and handling dependencies. Following this foundational knowledge, "Patterns for Effective Inter-service Communication" delves into the various methods for service-to-service interactions, such as synchronous RESTful APIs or asynchronous messaging patterns, weighing their benefits and drawbacks in different scenarios to help direct communication strategy selection.

As the architecture matures, "Implementing Service Discovery in Microservices" becomes critical for dynamically locating and engaging with services within the system. This recipe describes service discovery techniques and how to use them in a Go-based microservices framework. "Logging and Monitoring Microservices" highlights the need of observability in distributed systems, providing tools and procedures for collecting logs, metrics, and traces to monitor microservice health and performance.

Moving on to deployment problems, "Containerizing Microservices with Docker" shows how to package and execute microservices in containers, enabling uniform environments across development, testing, and production. Finally, "Orchestrating Microservices with Kubernetes" walks you through the process of managing and scaling containerized microservices, demonstrating Kubernetes' ability as an automated deployment, scaling, and administration tool for microservice applications.

By the end of this chapter, you will have a comprehensive understanding of building and managing microservices architectures using Go, prepared to tackle the complexities of modern, distributed applications with confidence and expertise.

Recipe 1: Designing and Implementing a Go Microservice

Understanding Microservice Architecture

Microservice architecture is a method of developing software systems that are divided into a collection of smaller, autonomous services. Each service is self-contained and implements a specific business function. This architecture style enables scalability, resilience, and faster development cycles. Microservices communicate with each other through well-defined APIs, often using lightweight protocols like HTTP/REST or messaging queues.

Practical Solution

Define the Service Boundaries

Start by identifying a distinct functionality or domain within your application. For example, a "Book Catalog" service in a library management system might be responsible for managing book information.

Set up the Go Microservice Project

Organize your Go project with a clean structure, separating your domain logic, API handlers, and external integrations.

/book-catalog

/cmd

main.go // Entry point for the microservice

/internal

/handlers // HTTP handlers for the web API

/domain // Domain model and business logic

/repository // Data access layer

/pkg

/api // API clients for other services

Implementing a Basic HTTP Server

Use the **net/http** package to set up an HTTP server. This will serve as the interface for the microservice.

```go
package main

import (
    "log"
    "net/http"
)

func main() {
    http.HandleFunc("/books", bookHandler)
    log.Println("Book Catalog service listening on port 8080")
    log.Fatal(http.ListenAndServe(":8080", nil))
}

func bookHandler(w http.ResponseWriter, r *http.Request) {
    // Handler logic to interact with the book catalog
}
```

Define Domain Models and Business Logic

In the **/internal/domain** directory, define your business entities and logic. This encapsulates the core functionality of your microservice.

```go
package domain

type Book struct {
    ID string `json:"id"`
    Title string `json:"title"`
    Author string `json:"author"`
```

}

// Example business logic function

```go
func (b *Book) UpdateTitle(newTitle string) {
  b.Title = newTitle
}
```

Data Access Layer

Implement data access logic in the **/internal/repository** directory. This layer interacts with the database or storage backend.

```go
package repository

import "context"

type BookRepository interface {
  FindByID(ctx context.Context, id string) (*domain.Book, error)
  // Other data access methods
}
```

Microservices Communication

For microservices to interact, define clear APIs using protocols like HTTP/REST for synchronous calls or message brokers for asynchronous communication. This ensures loose coupling and service autonomy.

You can design and implement a focused, scalable, and maintainable Go microservice by adhering to this recipe. By following microservices best practices and laying out your project explicitly, you can make sure that each service can adapt on its own, which is good for agile development and deployment.

Recipe 2: Achieving Effective Inter-service Communication

Challenges in Inter-service Communication

Services in a microservices architecture must exchange messages in order to carry out tasks that cross over into other services. Issues including network latency, message formatting, and error handling complicate what should be an efficient, dependable, and secure communication process. Considerations like real-time responses and background processing should direct the choice of communication protocol and pattern (synchronous vs. asynchronous).

Practical Solution

HTTP/REST is widely used for synchronous communication due to its simplicity and compatibility with web standards.

Implementing a REST Client with Go

Use Go's **net/http** package to create a REST client. This client can consume services by making HTTP requests and processing responses.

```go
package main

import (
    "bytes"
    "encoding/json"
    "io/ioutil"
    "log"
    "net/http"
)

type Book struct {
    ID string `json:"id"`
    Title string `json:"title"`
    Author string `json:"author"`
}
```

```go
func getBookDetails(serviceURL, bookID string) (*Book, error) {
    resp, err := http.Get(serviceURL + "/books/" + bookID)
    if err != nil {
        return nil, err
    }
    defer resp.Body.Close()
    body, err := ioutil.ReadAll(resp.Body)
    if err != nil {
        return nil, err
    }
    var book Book
    if err := json.Unmarshal(body, &book); err != nil {
        return nil, err
    }
    return &book, nil
}
```

For operations that don't require an immediate response, or to decouple service dependencies further, asynchronous communication via messaging queues or brokers is effective.

Implementing a Messaging Client

Use a messaging system like RabbitMQ, Kafka, or NATS.

Following is a simplified example with a hypothetical messaging library:

```go
package main
```

```go
import (
    "log"
    "messaging"
)

func publishBookUpdate(book Book) {
    if err := messaging.Publish("book-updates", book); err != nil {
        log.Fatalf("Failed to publish book update: %v", err)
    }
}

func subscribeToBookUpdates() {
    updates, err := messaging.Subscribe("book-updates")
    if err != nil {
        log.Fatalf("Failed to subscribe to book updates: %v", err)
    }
    for update := range updates {
        log.Printf("Received book update: %v", update)
        // Process update
    }
}
```

Choosing the Right Pattern

The choice between synchronous and asynchronous communication depends on the specific requirements of your interaction. Synchronous communication, while simpler, introduces direct dependencies between services. Asynchronous communication, using messaging systems, reduces these dependencies and can improve scalability but may introduce complexity in message handling and processing.

Recipe 3: Implementing Service Discovery in Microservices

Situation

In order to function properly, microservices must be able to dynamically learn where other services on the network are located. The fleeting nature of service instances makes hard-coded or statically configured endpoints unworkable in scalable and cloud-based setups. Ensuring services can find and communicate with one other as they dynamically scale up or down is the main problem of creating a reliable and effective service discovery mechanism.

Practical Solution

Service discovery can be categorized into two main patterns: client-side discovery and server-side discovery. In this situation, we focus on client-side discovery, where the service client retrieves information from a service registry and uses it to make direct calls to the service.

Using a Service Registry

A service registry is a database of services, their instances, and their locations. Services register themselves with the registry on startup and deregister on shutdown. Clients query the registry to find the services they need.

Consul by HashiCorp is a popular choice for service discovery, providing a distributed, highly available, and datacenter-aware registry.

Registering a Service with Consul in Go

When a service starts, it should register itself with Consul. Use the **consul/api** package to interact with Consul from Go.

```
import (

"github.com/hashicorp/consul/api"

"log"

)
```

```go
func registerServiceWithConsul() {

    config := api.DefaultConfig()

    consul, err := api.NewClient(config)

    if err != nil {

    log.Fatalf("Consul client error: %s", err)

    }

    registration := new(api.AgentServiceRegistration)

    registration.ID = "book-service-1" // Unique service ID

    registration.Name = "book-service"

    registration.Port = 8080

    registration.Tags = []string{"urlprefix-/books strip=/books"}

    registration.Address = "127.0.0.1"

    err = consul.Agent().ServiceRegister(registration)

    if err != nil {

    log.Fatalf("Failed to register with Consul: %s", err)

    }
}
```

Discovering Services with Consul in Go

Clients use the Consul API to discover the location of services.

```go
func discoverService(serviceName string) {

    config := api.DefaultConfig()
```

```
consul, err := api.NewClient(config)

if err != nil {

log.Fatalf("Consul client error: %s", err)

}

services, _, err := consul.Health().Service(serviceName, "", true, nil)

if err != nil {

log.Fatalf("Service discovery failed: %s", err)

}

for _, service := range services {

log.Printf("Discovered service: %v at %v:%v\n", service.Service.Service, service.Service.Address, service.Service.Port)

// Use the service address and port

}

}
```

Implementing service discovery enables microservices to dynamically locate and communicate with each other, addressing the challenges of service location in distributed systems. By leveraging tools like Consul, microservices can maintain up-to-date knowledge of the network topology, ensuring resilient and efficient inter-service communication.

Recipe 4: Logging and Monitoring Microservices

Scenario

Imagine deploying several microservices that interact to form a complex application. Over time, you notice sporadic performance dips and occasional failures in specific services, affecting user experience. The challenge here is not only to pinpoint the root cause of these issues across multiple services but also to proactively monitor the system's health to prevent future disruptions.

Practical Solution

Implement a centralized logging system where all microservices can send their logs. This approach simplifies log analysis and debugging across services.

Using Logrus with a Log Aggregator

Logrus is a structured logger for Go, offering more flexibility than the standard library's logging package. When used in conjunction with a log aggregator like ELK (Elasticsearch, Logstash, Kibana) or Loki, it can significantly enhance log management.

```go
import (

"github.com/sirupsen/logrus"

)

func setupLogger() *logrus.Logger {

logger := logrus.New()

logger.Formatter = &logrus.JSONFormatter{} // Structured logging

// Configure log level, output, etc.

return logger

}

// Example usage

logger := setupLogger()

logger.Info("Microservice starting up", logrus.Fields{"service": "user-auth", "port": 8080})
```

Monitoring with Prometheus and Grafana

Prometheus is an open-source monitoring solution that collects and stores metrics as time series data. Grafana can then visualize this data, providing insights into the application's performance and health.

Add Prometheus metrics to your Go microservices. This involves importing the Prometheus client library and exposing a metrics endpoint.

```
import (
 "github.com/prometheus/client_golang/prometheus"
 "github.com/prometheus/client_golang/prometheus/promhttp"
 "net/http"
)
func main() {
 http.Handle("/metrics", promhttp.Handler())
 // Register custom metrics
 http.ListenAndServe(":9090", nil) // Expose the metrics on port 9090
}
```

Visualizing Metrics with Grafana

Connect Grafana to your Prometheus data source to create dashboards that visualize key performance indicators (KPIs) for your microservices, such as request rates, error rates, and response times.

You can see how well your microservices are doing by using Logrus for structured logging and centralized log aggregation, plus Prometheus and Grafana for thorough monitoring. You can fix problems fast, maximize performance, and keep service reliability and user happiness high with this configuration.

Recipe 5: Containerizing Microservices with Docker

Scenario

You've built a microservice that serves as the backend of your application and it runs smoothly on your local PC. It works OK in your local environment, but fails when deployed to a server. Your requirement for a solution to encapsulate your microservice and its dependencies has become apparent, and you want to find a way to make sure it works consistently in every scenario

Practical Solution

Installing Docker

If Docker is not already installed on your Linux system, you can install it by following these steps. Make sure that the exact commands might vary based on your Linux distribution.

sudo apt update

sudo apt install apt-transport-https ca-certificates curl software-properties-common

curl -fsSL https://download.docker.com/linux/ubuntu/gpg | sudo apt-key add -

sudo add-apt-repository "deb [arch=amd64] https://download.docker.com/linux/ubuntu $(lsb_release -cs) stable"

sudo apt update

sudo apt install docker-ce

Verify the installation

sudo systemctl status docker

Creating a Dockerfile

For your microservice, create a **Dockerfile** in the root of your project. This file contains instructions for building your Docker image.

Use an official Go runtime as a parent image

FROM golang:1.15 as builder

Set the working directory in the container

WORKDIR /app

Copy the current directory contents into the container at /app

COPY . .

Download all dependencies

RUN go mod download

Build the Go app

RUN CGO_ENABLED=0 GOOS=linux go build -a -installsuffix cgo -o myservice .

Use a small Alpine Linux image for the final build

FROM alpine:latest

RUN apk --no-cache add ca-certificates

WORKDIR /root/

Copy the binary from the builder stage

COPY --from=builder /app/myservice .

Expose port 8080 to the outside world

EXPOSE 8080

Command to run the executable

CMD ["./myservice"]

Building and Running Your Docker Container

With the **Dockerfile** created, you can now build the Docker image for your microservice and run it as a container.
Build the image:

```
docker build -t myservice .
```

Run the container

```
docker run -d -p 8080:8080 myservice
```

This command runs your microservice in a container, mapping port 8080 of the container to port 8080 on the host, making your service accessible.

Docker containerization wraps your microservice and its environment, making it run consistently across deployments. Our technique streamlines application deployment, scaling, and management, resulting in a more resilient and portable application.

Recipe 6: Orchestrating Microservices with Kubernetes

Scenario

Orchestrating microservices efficiently is crucial for managing their lifecycle, scaling, and ensuring high availability. Since kubernetes emerges as a powerful system for automating deployment, scaling, and operations of application containers across clusters of hosts, we must learn to use kubernetes for orchestrating microservices.

Setting up a Kubernetes Cluster

If Kubernetes is not set up, you can create a local cluster for development purposes using Minikube. Minikube runs a single-node Kubernetes cluster inside a VM on your laptop.

Install Minikube

For Linux environments, you can install Minikube directly. Ensure you have a virtualization provider like VirtualBox or KVM installed.

```
curl -Lo minikube https://storage.googleapis.com/minikube/releases/latest/minikube-linux-amd64
```

```
chmod +x minikube
```

```
sudo mv minikube /usr/local/bin/
```

Start Minikube

Initialize the cluster with the **minikube start** command. This sets up a basic Kubernetes cluster.

```
minikube start
```

Verify Installation

Ensure that Kubernetes is correctly installed by checking the cluster status.

```
kubectl cluster-info
```

Deploying a Microservice to Kubernetes

With the Kubernetes cluster ready, you can deploy your containerized microservice.

Create a Deployment Configuration

Define a Kubernetes Deployment that manages your microservice's deployment. Save this configuration in a file named **myservice-deployment.yaml**.

```
apiVersion: apps/v1

kind: Deployment

metadata:

 name: myservice-deployment

spec:

 replicas: 2

 selector:

 matchLabels:

 app: myservice

 template:

 metadata:

 labels:
```

```
      app: myservice
  spec:
    containers:
    - name: myservice
      image: myservice:latest
      ports:
      - containerPort: 8080
```

Deploy Your Microservice
Apply the deployment configuration to your cluster.

```
kubectl apply -f myservice-deployment.yaml
```

Expose Your Microservice
After deployment, expose your microservice externally through a Kubernetes Service.

```
kubectl expose deployment myservice-deployment --type=LoadBalancer --name=myservice-service --port=8080
```

Accessing Your Service
If you are using Minikube, you can access your service using the **minikube service** command.

```
minikube service myservice-service
```

Best Practices for Kubernetes
- Ensure your container images are lightweight and secure.
- Use Kubernetes namespaces to isolate environments within the same cluster.
- Implement health checks in your deployments to enhance service reliability.

Summary

In this chapter, we covered all the bases of using Go for microservice development, deployment, and management, with an emphasis on best practices for scalability, maintainability, and operability. Beginning with the design and execution of individual microservices, this chapter establishes the framework for understanding the principles of the microservices architecture, with a focus on designing services that are cohesive, loosely connected, and deployable independently. This foundation is critical for you to understand the granularity, autonomy, and distributed nature of microservices, allowing you to create services that accurately target specific business capabilities while ensuring easy development and deployment.

As the chapter develops, it goes deeper into the complexities of microservices architecture, including effective inter-service communication, service discovery, logging, monitoring, Docker containerization, and Kubernetes orchestration. These recipes address the issues of managing several interacting services, particularly in cloud and dynamic contexts where services are often scaled up and down. Effective inter-service communication and service discovery are emphasized as critical for allowing services to locate and talk with one another seamlessly. Meanwhile, logging and monitoring are emphasized as critical to operational visibility and troubleshooting. The containerization and orchestration sections explain how Docker and Kubernetes can be used to encapsulate microservices, manage their lifecycle, and automate deployment and scaling, resulting in a strong infrastructure that supports the dynamic nature of microservices.

By the end of this chapter, you will have the knowledge and tools you need to construct, implement, and manage microservices in Go, preparing you to face the challenges of modern, distributed applications. This journey through microservices architecture with Go not only improves your ability to construct scalable and resilient systems, but also prepares you to traverse the changing terrain of cloud-native development with confidence and knowledge.

CHAPTER 8:
STRENGTHENING DATABASE INTERACTIONS

Introduction

This chapter is all about improving the methods for working with databases in Go apps and getting a better grasp on how they work. This chapter covers the fundamentals of database operations, such as connection establishment, sophisticated query execution, and performance optimization. It is designed to provide you with a comprehensive toolkit for properly managing data, ensuring that applications are scalable, resilient, and efficient.

We will start with "Establishing SQL Database Connectivity in Go," which will teach you the fundamentals of any database-driven program. This includes configuring connections to SQL databases and knowing the nuances of connection pooling in order to efficiently manage resources. Moving on, "Executing CRUD Operations with Go and SQL" delves into the fundamentals of database interaction, demonstrating how to create, read, update, and delete records with precision and efficiency, ensuring that you understand the core operations that underpin most applications.

The adventure continues with "Leveraging ORM Tools for Database Interaction," which introduces Object-Relational Mapping (ORM) as a powerful paradigm for abstracting and simplifying database interactions, minimizing boilerplate, and enhancing code maintainability. "Advanced Transaction Handling and Concurrency" focuses on more complex scenarios, assuring data integrity and consistency throughout concurrent processes, which is crucial in high-traffic systems.

As we progress through "Working with NoSQL Databases in Go Applications," the chapter looks beyond SQL to schema-less data stores and their flexibility and scalability benefits. "Advanced Query Techniques for Data Retrieval" and "Performing Effective Database Migrations" expand on the skillset by learning sophisticated querying strategies and safe schema evolution practices. Finally, "Implementing High-Performance Database Caching" concludes the chapter by learning caching solutions for improving application performance, lowering latency, and minimizing database load.

This chapter, using actual examples and extensive explanations, enables you to confidently navigate the complicated environment of database interactions, guaranteeing you can construct data-driven Go apps that are not only functional but also optimized for performance and scalability.

Recipe 1: Establishing SQL Database Connectivity in Go

Scenario

Imagine you are developing a part of an application that requires storing and retrieving user information. To handle this data efficiently, you decide to use PostgreSQL. The initial challenge is to establish a stable connection between your Go application and the PostgreSQL database, enabling you to perform further database operations seamlessly.

Practical Solution

Install PostgreSQL Driver

To interact with PostgreSQL from Go, you need a driver. We will use **pq**, a popular driver for PostgreSQL. Install it using:

go get -u github.com/lib/pq

Set up Database Connection

Use the **database/sql** package in Go, which provides a generic interface around SQL (or SQL-like) databases, in combination with the **pq** driver to establish a connection. Create a function to connect to the database:

package main

import (

"database/sql"

"fmt"

"log"

_ "github.com/lib/pq"

)

const (

host = "localhost"

port = 5432 // Default port for PostgreSQL

user = "yourusername"

password = "yourpassword"

```go
    dbname = "yourdbname"
)

func connectDB() *sql.DB {
    psqlInfo := fmt.Sprintf("host=%s port=%d user=%s "+
        "password=%s dbname=%s sslmode=disable",
        host, port, user, password, dbname)
    db, err := sql.Open("postgres", psqlInfo)
    if err != nil {
        log.Fatalf("Error connecting to the database: %v", err)
    }
    err = db.Ping()
    if err != nil {
        log.Fatalf("Error pinging the database: %v", err)
    }
    fmt.Println("Successfully connected!")
    return db
}

func main() {
    db := connectDB()
    defer db.Close()
    // Further operations...
```

}

Understanding the Connection String

The connection string (**psqlInfo**) includes several parameters essential for connecting to the PostgreSQL database, such as the host, port, username, password, and database name. The **sslmode=disable** parameter is used here for simplicity, but for production environments, consider enabling SSL mode for security.

Testing the Connection

The **db.Ping()** method is used to test the connectivity with the database server. It's a good practice to verify the connection as part of the initialization process to ensure your application can communicate with the database before proceeding with further operations.

By establishing a connection to a PostgreSQL database, your Go application gains the ability to interact with persistent storage, opening up possibilities for creating, reading, updating, and deleting data as required by your application's functionality.

Recipe 2: Executing CRUD Operations with Go and SQL

Scenario

We will assume you need to manage user information within your application. This requires capabilities to add new users, retrieve user details, update user information, and delete users from your PostgreSQL database.

Practical Solution

Using the **database/sql** package in Go, you can execute SQL queries to perform these CRUD operations.

Following is how you can implement each operation:

Create (Inserting Data)

Add a new user to the database.

```
func createUser(db *sql.DB, name, email string) error {

    query := `INSERT INTO users (name, email) VALUES ($1, $2)`
```

```go
_, err := db.Exec(query, name, email)
if err != nil {
return err
}
fmt.Println("User added successfully")
return nil
}
```

Read (Querying Data)

Retrieve details of a specific user by email.

```go
type User struct {
ID int
Name string
Email string
}
func getUserByEmail(db *sql.DB, email string) (*User, error) {
query := `SELECT id, name, email FROM users WHERE email = $1`
var user User
row := db.QueryRow(query, email)
err := row.Scan(&user.ID, &user.Name, &user.Email)
if err != nil {
if err == sql.ErrNoRows {
```

```go
        return nil, fmt.Errorf("user not found")
    }
    return nil, err
}
return &user, nil
}
```

Update (Modifying Data)

Update the name of a user based on their email.

```go
func updateUserEmail(db *sql.DB, id int, newEmail string) error {
    query := `UPDATE users SET email = $2 WHERE id = $1`
    _, err := db.Exec(query, id, newEmail)
    if err != nil {
        return err
    }
    fmt.Println("User email updated successfully")
    return nil
}
```

Delete (Removing Data)

Remove a user from the database.

```go
func deleteUser(db *sql.DB, id int) error {
    query := `DELETE FROM users WHERE id = $1`
```

```go
_, err := db.Exec(query, id)

if err != nil {

return err

}

fmt.Println("User deleted successfully")

return nil

}
```

Best Practices

- Use parameterized queries (**$1, $2**, etc.) to prevent SQL injection.
- Handle potential errors, including checking for **sql.ErrNoRows** when querying for a single row.
- Consider using transactions for operations that need to execute multiple steps atomically.

Recipe 3: Leveraging ORM Tools for Database Interaction

Scenario

Consider an application that requires frequent and complex interactions with a user database. Writing and maintaining raw SQL queries for these interactions becomes cumbersome and error-prone. By leveraging an ORM tool, you can streamline these operations, focusing on business logic rather than database specifics.

Practical Solution

One popular ORM tool in the Go ecosystem is GORM. It offers a developer-friendly API for performing CRUD operations and more, with support for various SQL databases including PostgreSQL, MySQL, SQLite, and SQL Server.

Installing GORM

To get started with GORM, first install it by running:

go get -u gorm.io/gorm

go get -u gorm.io/driver/postgres

Connecting to the Database

Use GORM to establish a connection to your PostgreSQL database.

```go
package main

import (
    "gorm.io/driver/postgres"
    "gorm.io/gorm"
    "log"
)

func main() {
    dsn := "host=localhost user=youruser password=yourpassword dbname=yourdbname port=5432 sslmode=disable TimeZone=Asia/Shanghai"
    db, err := gorm.Open(postgres.Open(dsn), &gorm.Config{})
    if err != nil {
        log.Fatalf("Failed to connect to database: %v", err)
    }
    log.Println("Database connection successfully established")
}
```

Defining a Model

Create a Go struct that maps to your database table. GORM uses this model to perform database operations.

```go
type User struct {
    gorm.Model
    Name string
    Email string `gorm:"type:varchar(100);unique_index"`
}
```

Performing CRUD Operations

With GORM, executing CRUD operations becomes straightforward. Following is how you can add a new user to the database:

```go
newUser := User{Name: "John Doe", Email: "john.doe@example.com"}
result := db.Create(&newUser) // Pass pointer of data to Create
if result.Error != nil {
    log.Fatalf("Failed to create user: %v", result.Error)
}
log.Printf("User created successfully: %v", newUser)
```

Similarly, you can use **db.Find**, **db.Update**, and **db.Delete** for read, update, and delete operations, respectively.

Benefits of Using an ORM

- Abstraction over SQL: ORM allows you to focus on your application's business logic rather than the intricacies of SQL syntax.
- Type Safety: Working with Go structs instead of raw queries reduces the risk of runtime errors and SQL injection vulnerabilities.
- Development Speed: ORM can accelerate development by automating routine data handling tasks, such as migrations and query optimizations.

Recipe 4: Advanced Transaction Handling and

Concurrency

Scenario

Try to picture a program that takes orders and keeps stock levels up to date. It is possible for numerous users to try to buy the same item at the same time during a sale event. To avoid data anomalies like selling more items than in stock, strong transaction handling is necessary to update inventory levels accurately in this case.

Practical Solution

Using Transactions in Go

Database transactions ensure that a series of operations either all succeed or fail as a unit, maintaining data integrity. Go's **database/sql** package supports transactions.

```go
func processOrder(db *sql.DB, orderID, itemID int, quantity int) error {

    // Begin a transaction

    tx, err := db.Begin()

    if err != nil {

        return err

    }

    // Deduct the quantity from inventory

    _, err = tx.Exec("UPDATE inventory SET quantity = quantity - ? WHERE item_id = ?", quantity, itemID)

    if err != nil {

        tx.Rollback() // Important: Rollback in case of error

        return err

    }
```

```go
// Update order status
_, err = tx.Exec("UPDATE orders SET status = 'processed' WHERE id = ?", orderID)
if err != nil {
    tx.Rollback() // Rollback in case of error
    return err
}
// Commit the transaction
if err := tx.Commit(); err != nil {
    return err
}
return nil
}
```

Handling Concurrency

Optimistic and pessimistic locking are two strategies to handle concurrency. Optimistic locking assumes conflicts are rare, while pessimistic locking assumes conflicts are common and locks data to prevent other operations from accessing it simultaneously.

Implement optimistic locking by including a version or timestamp column in your table. When updating a record, check that the version matches, indicating no other transactions have modified the record.

```sql
UPDATE inventory SET quantity = quantity - ?, version = version + 1 WHERE item_id = ? AND version = ?
```

If the update affects 0 rows, it means another transaction has already updated the record, and you can handle this case accordingly (e.g., retry the operation, abort, or notify the user).

Best Practices

- Always use transactions for groups of operations that must be executed together.
- Be mindful of the potential for deadlocks and design your database access patterns to minimize this risk.
- Regularly review and optimize your transaction handling and concurrency control mechanisms, especially as your application scales and evolves.

Recipe 5: Working with NoSQL Databases - MongoDB Integration

Scenario

The library application needs to store and retrieve user reviews for books, where reviews can vary significantly in structure, containing comments, ratings, and potentially user metadata. This scenario is well-suited for a NoSQL database like MongoDB due to its schema-less nature and flexibility.

Practical Solution

Setting up MongoDB in Go

To interact with MongoDB from Go, use the official MongoDB Go driver. First, add the MongoDB Go driver to your project:

go get go.mongodb.org/mongo-driver/mongo

Connecting to MongoDB

Establish a connection to your MongoDB instance. The below sample program assumes MongoDB is running locally on the default port and uses a new database called **librarydb**.

package main

import (

 "context"

 "log"

 "time"

```go
    "go.mongodb.org/mongo-driver/mongo"
    "go.mongodb.org/mongo-driver/mongo/options"
)

func main() {

    // Set client options

    clientOptions := options.Client().ApplyURI("mongodb://localhost:27017")

    // Connect to MongoDB

    client, err := mongo.Connect(context.TODO(), clientOptions)

    if err != nil {

    log.Fatal(err)

    }

    // Check the connection

    err = client.Ping(context.TODO(), nil)

    if err != nil {

    log.Fatal(err)

    }

    log.Println("Connected to MongoDB!")

}
```

Defining a Model for User Reviews

Since MongoDB is schema-less, you can define a flexible Go struct that represents a user review. This struct can then be used to marshal and unmarshal data to and from MongoDB.

```go
type UserReview struct {
    ID primitive.ObjectID `bson:"_id,omitempty"`
    BookID string `bson:"book_id"`
    UserID string `bson:"user_id"`
    Rating int `bson:"rating"`
    Comment string `bson:"comment,omitempty"`
}
```

Performing CRUD Operations

With the connection established and model defined, you can now perform CRUD operations. Given below is how to insert a new review into the database:

```go
func createReview(client *mongo.Client, review UserReview) error {
    collection := client.Database("librarydb").Collection("reviews")
    _, err := collection.InsertOne(context.TODO(), review)
    if err != nil {
        return err
    }
    log.Println("Review inserted successfully")
    return nil
}
```

Best Practices

- Use context to manage timeouts and cancellations for database operations.
- Regularly update your MongoDB driver to benefit from the latest features and improvements.

- Consider indexing your collections based on query patterns to improve performance.

Recipe 6: Executing Advanced Query Techniques for Insightful Data Retrieval

Scenario

In the evolving library application, there is a need to offer users personalized book recommendations based on their reading history, preferences, and reviews by similar users. This requirement calls for advanced querying capabilities to analyze user data, book metadata, and interaction patterns to generate meaningful recommendations.

Practical Solution

Using PostgreSQL for structured data and MongoDB for user-generated content like reviews, we can employ advanced query techniques in both SQL and NoSQL environments to achieve our goal.

SQL Window Functions in PostgreSQL

Window functions provide a way to perform calculations across sets of rows related to the current row. This can be used for ranking, running totals, or identifying patterns.

For example, to find the top 3 most popular books in a category based on checkout history:

```
SELECT book_id, category, COUNT(*) OVER (PARTITION BY category ORDER BY COUNT(*) DESC) as checkout_count

FROM checkouts

WHERE checkout_date > CURRENT_DATE - INTERVAL '1 year'

GROUP BY book_id, category

ORDER BY category, checkout_count DESC

LIMIT 3;
```

Aggregation Pipeline in MongoDB

MongoDB's aggregation framework allows for data processing and aggregation through a multistage pipeline, enabling complex data transformations and analysis.

For instance, to aggregate user reviews for generating book ratings:

```
collection := client.Database("librarydb").Collection("reviews")

pipeline := mongo.Pipeline{

 {{"$match", bson.D{{"book_id", bookID}}}},

 {{"$group", bson.D{

 {"_id", "$book_id"},

 {"average_rating", bson.D{{"$avg", "$rating"}}},

 }}},

}

aggResult, err := collection.Aggregate(context.TODO(), pipeline)

if err != nil {

 log.Fatal(err)

}

// Process aggregation results
```

Combining SQL and NoSQL Queries for Data Insights

By leveraging the strengths of both SQL and NoSQL databases, you can perform sophisticated data analysis. For instance, use SQL queries to analyze transactional data and user interactions stored in PostgreSQL, and MongoDB's aggregation pipeline to analyze user-generated content. The insights from both sources can be combined to power features like personalized recommendations or trend analysis.

Best Practices

- Always index your database based on the query patterns to optimize query performance.
- Regularly review and refactor your queries as your application and its data grow in complexity.

- For MongoDB, consider using the **$lookup** stage in your aggregation pipelines for performing joins with other collections when necessary.

Recipe 7: Performing Effective Database Migrations

Scenario

Adding new tables to keep track of book reservations or modifying existing tables to fit additional data fields for user profiles are examples of database schema modifications that may be necessary as the library application develops and gets new capabilities. A solid migration plan is required to implement these changes in all environments (dev, test, and production) without disrupting service or losing data.

Practical Solution

Choosing a Migration Tool

For Go applications, several tools facilitate database migrations, such as **golang-migrate/migrate**. This tool supports various databases and allows you to define migrations in SQL or Go files.

```
go get -u github.com/golang-migrate/migrate/cmd/migrate
```

Creating Migration Scripts

Migrations usually consist of two scripts: one for applying the change ("up") and one for undoing the change ("down"), allowing you to roll back to a previous state if necessary.

Example Migration for Adding a Reservations Table:

Create a directory for your migration files, e.g., **migrations**, and then create an "up" migration file for creating a new table:

1_add_reservations_table.up.sql

```sql
CREATE TABLE reservations (
  id SERIAL PRIMARY KEY,
  user_id INTEGER NOT NULL,
```

    book_id INTEGER NOT NULL,

    reserved_at TIMESTAMP WITH TIME ZONE DEFAULT CURRENT TIMESTAMP

);

And a corresponding "down" migration file to undo the change:

1_add_reservations_table.down.sql

DROP TABLE reservations;

Use the **migrate** tool to apply your migrations to the database. Specify the database connection string and the path to your migrations directory.

Applying Migrations

```
migrate -path /path/to/migrations -database "postgres://user:password@localhost:5432/dbname?sslmode=disable" up
```

Rolling Back Migrations

```
migrate -path /path/to/migrations -database "postgres://user:password@localhost:5432/dbname?sslmode=disable" down
```

Best Practices

- Always test migrations in a development or staging environment before applying them to production.
- Maintain a clear naming convention for migration files that indicates the sequence and purpose of each migration.
- Include comprehensive "down" migrations to ensure that any changes can be safely reverted.

Recipe 8: Implementing High-Performance Database Caching

Scenario

In the library application, certain operations, such as fetching popular books or user profiles, are executed frequently and generate similar queries to the database. To optimize these operations, implementing a caching layer can reduce direct database queries, lowering latency and improving throughput, especially under high load.

Practical Solution

Redis is a popular in-memory data store used as a high-performance cache and message broker. It offers various data structures to efficiently cache different types of data.

Setting up Redis

Ensure Redis is installed and running on your system. Redis can be easily set up on most platforms, and Docker can be used to run Redis in a container for development purposes.

Integrating Redis with Go

Use the **go-redis/redis** Go client to interact with Redis from your application.

```
go get -u github.com/go-redis/redis/v8
```

Establish a connection to your Redis instance.

```go
package main

import (
    "context"
    "fmt"
    "github.com/go-redis/redis/v8"
)

var ctx = context.Background()

func main() {
    rdb := redis.NewClient(&redis.Options{
```

```go
        Addr:     "localhost:6379", // use default Addr
        Password: "",               // no password set
        DB:       0,                // use default DB
    })
    err := rdb.Set(ctx, "key", "value", 0).Err()
    if err != nil {
        panic(err)
    }
    val, err := rdb.Get(ctx, "key").Result()
    if err != nil {
        panic(err)
    }
    fmt.Println("key", val)
}
```

Caching Strategy for Frequently Accessed Data

Implement caching logic in your application to store and retrieve frequently accessed data. For read-heavy operations, retrieve the data from the cache if available; if not, fetch from the database and store it in the cache for future requests.

```go
func getPopularBooks(rdb *redis.Client, db *sql.DB) ([]Book, error) {
    // Attempt to fetch the value from Redis cache
    cachedBooks, err := rdb.Get(ctx, "popular_books").Result()
    if err == redis.Nil {
```

```go
// Key does not exist in Redis, fetch from database
books, err := fetchPopularBooksFromDB(db)
if err != nil {
    return nil, err
}
// Cache the result in Redis
if err := rdb.Set(ctx, "popular_books", books, 30*time.Minute).Err(); err != nil {
    // handle error
}
return books, nil
} else if err != nil {
    return nil, err
}
// Unmarshal the data into the expected slice of books
var books []Book
if err := json.Unmarshal([]byte(cachedBooks), &books); err != nil {
    return nil, err
}
return books, nil
}
```

Best Practices

- Use appropriate expiration times for cached data to ensure it remains fresh.
- Handle cache failures gracefully to ensure the application can still serve data by falling back to the database.
- Monitor cache hit rates and adjust your caching strategy as needed to maximize efficiency.

Summary

In this chapter, we looked at ways to make database operations in Go apps more efficient and reliable. Beginning with connecting to SQL databases, the chapter advances to performing basic CRUD tasks, emphasizing the importance of direct SQL interactions for exact data manipulation. The investigation into using ORM tools like as GORM for database interactions highlights a trend toward more abstracted, developer-friendly techniques that enable fast database management while reducing boilerplate code. This combination of direct and ORM-based interactions offers you with a comprehensive toolkit for database operations, catering to a wide range of application requirements and complexity levels.

Advanced topics like transaction handling, concurrency control, and working with NoSQL databases like MongoDB broaden the developer's toolkit, addressing circumstances that necessitate advanced data integrity controls and flexible data models. Advanced query techniques, including as window functions and aggregation pipelines, enable more insightful data retrieval while also providing complicated analytical and reporting functionalities. Furthermore, the discussion of performing effective database migrations and implementing high-speed caching with Redis encompasses the entire lifecycle and optimization of database interactions, highlighting approaches that assure data consistency, application scalability, and performance. This chapter provides you with the knowledge and skills you need to navigate the complexities of database integration, from initial setup and CRUD operations to advanced optimization and scaling techniques, ensuring that Go applications are efficient, scalable, and maintainable.

Chapter 9: Enhancing Performance and Best Practices in Go

Introduction

Optimization of Go applications for efficiency, speed, and maintainability is the main focus of this chapter. This chapter is designed to improve Go developers' skills by delving into strategies for writing high-performance code, identifying and addressing performance bottlenecks, effectively managing memory, using design patterns to solve common problems elegantly, and handling dependencies with precision. The chapter's goal is to provide you with the information you need to construct strong, efficient, and scalable Go programs by combining theory with practical examples.

The adventure begins with "Writing High-Performance Go Code," where we examine the characteristics of performant Go code, including idiomatic patterns, concurrency models, and recommended practices that take advantage of Go's capabilities. This foundation lays the groundwork for the following recipe, "Profiling Go Applications for Performance Tuning," which covers tools and strategies for profiling Go apps. You will learn how to use profiling to get insights into CPU utilization, memory allocation, and other key performance parameters, allowing for targeted optimizations.

As we go on to "Achieving Efficient Memory Management," we will learn about Go's garbage collection mechanism and tactics for decreasing memory allocations, which can have a substantial impact on application speed and latency. This recipe focuses on real memory-efficient code writing techniques, such as object reuse and data structure optimization.

"Implementing Design Patterns for Robust Go Code" investigates how existing design patterns can be adapted and applied in Go to tackle typical software design difficulties, resulting in code that is both efficient and maintainable. Finally, "Managing Dependencies and Go Modules Effectively" tackles the issues of dependency management in Go projects, guiding you through the usage of Go modules to ensure reliable and reproducible builds.

This chapter walks you through the art and science of performance optimization and best practices in Go, ensuring that your applications not only run well under load but are also designed for clarity, maintainability, and scalability.

Recipe 1: Writing High-Performance Go Code

Scenario

Consider the "Implementing High-Performance Database Caching" recipe from Chapter 8, where we introduced caching with Redis to optimize database interactions. This scenario highlighted the importance of reducing database load and improving response times. Building on this, we will explore how to write more performant Go code by optimizing a function that processes and caches book data, ensuring minimal latency and efficient resource usage.

Practical Solution

Avoid Unnecessary Memory Allocations

Reducing memory allocations can significantly improve performance, especially in hot code paths. Use buffer pools and reuse objects where possible.

- Before Optimization:

```go
func processBooks(books []Book) {
    for _, book := range books {
        data, _ := json.Marshal(book) // Potential high memory allocation
        // Process data...
    }
}
```

- After Optimization:

```go
import "sync"

var bufferPool = sync.Pool{
    New: func() interface{} {
        return new(bytes.Buffer)
    },
}

func processBooksOptimized(books []Book) {
    for _, book := range books {
        buf := bufferPool.Get().(*bytes.Buffer)
        buf.Reset()
```

json.NewEncoder(buf).Encode(book) // Lower memory allocation

// Process data...

bufferPool.Put(buf)

}

}

Leverage Concurrency for Parallel Processing

Go's goroutines and channels offer a lightweight way to parallelize work that can be done concurrently, improving throughput.

- Example with added concurrency:

func processBooksConcurrently(books []Book) {

var wg sync.WaitGroup

bookChan := make(chan Book)

for i := 0; i < 4; i++ { // Number of workers

wg.Add(1)

go func() {

defer wg.Done()

for book := range bookChan {

buf := bufferPool.Get().(*bytes.Buffer)

buf.Reset()

json.NewEncoder(buf).Encode(book)

// Process data...

bufferPool.Put(buf)

```
    }
}()
}
for _, book := range books {
    bookChan <- book
}
close(bookChan)
wg.Wait()
}
```

Optimize Use of Interfaces and Reflection

Interfaces and reflection provide flexibility but can come at a performance cost. Avoid unnecessary use of interfaces and reflection in performance-critical code paths.

Best Practices

- Profile your code to identify bottlenecks using Go's built-in profiling tools (**pprof**).
- Write benchmarks using the **testing** package to measure the performance impact of optimizations.
- Regularly review and update dependencies to leverage performance improvements in libraries and the Go runtime.

You may design high-performance Go programs by optimizing memory allocations, utilizing concurrency, and reducing the use of interfaces and reflection. The journey from a simple implementation to a highly efficient version exemplifies how careful coding habits and a thorough awareness of Go's capabilities may result in considerable performance increases.

Recipe 2: Profiling Go Applications for Performance Tuning

Scenario

Continuing with our previous discussion on writing Go code with good speed, imagine that your library application has streamlined data processing and introduced caching. Despite these efforts, you note that the application's response times vary under heavy load, indicating that inefficiencies have not yet been addressed. To identify these issues, profiling the application and analyzing its runtime performance becomes critical.

Practical Solution

CPU Profiling

CPU profiling helps you understand where your application spends its time. Use the **net/http/pprof** package to start profiling.

- Adding CPU Profiling to Your Application:

Import **net/http/pprof** in your main package. This automatically registers pprof handlers with the default mux.

```
import (

_ "net/http/pprof"

"net/http"

)

func main() {

go func() {

log.Println(http.ListenAndServe("localhost:6060", nil))

}()

// Your application logic here

}
```

- Then, generate a CPU profile:

```
go tool pprof http://localhost:6060/debug/pprof/profile?seconds=30
```

This command fetches a 30-second CPU profile from your running application and opens the pprof console for analysis.

Memory Profiling

Memory profiling identifies where your application allocates memory, helping to reduce overall memory usage and garbage collection pressure.

Similar to CPU profiling, you can fetch a memory profile through the pprof HTTP endpoint:

```
go tool pprof http://localhost:6060/debug/pprof/heap
```

Analyze the profile to identify areas with high memory allocation.

Block and Goroutine Profiling

Block profiling shows where goroutines block on synchronization primitives (e.g., mutex locks), and goroutine profiling provides a snapshot of all goroutines in the system.

- Enabling Block Profiling:

To enable block profiling, add runtime setup in your application:

```
import "runtime"

func main() {

runtime.SetBlockProfileRate(1)

// Your application setup

}
```

Fetch the block profile:

```
go tool pprof http://localhost:6060/debug/pprof/block
```

- Goroutine Profiling:

Goroutine profiles can be fetched directly without additional setup, similar to CPU and memory profiles.

Best Practices

- Regularly profile your application under different conditions to understand its behavior under load.
- Focus on optimizing the most resource-intensive parts of your application first, as identified by profiling.
- Use profiling in combination with benchmarks to measure the impact of your optimizations.

Recipe 3: Achieving Efficient Memory Management

Scenario

Imagine, for the sake of argument, that profiling has shown that memory allocation is a major bottleneck in our attempts to improve the library application. Frequent garbage collection cycles, caused by high memory utilization, result in visible increases in delay. We need to implement measures to control memory usage more effectively and decrease needless allocations to fix issues.

Practical Solution

Pooling and reusing objects can drastically reduce the need for new allocations, thereby lowering GC pressure.

Implementing Object Pooling

The **sync.Pool** type provides a convenient and thread-safe way to pool objects.

```
var bufferPool = sync.Pool{

 New: func() interface{} {

 return new(bytes.Buffer)

},

}

func getBuffer() *bytes.Buffer {

 return bufferPool.Get().(*bytes.Buffer)

}
```

```go
func putBuffer(buf *bytes.Buffer) {
    buf.Reset()
    bufferPool.Put(buf)
}
```

Use this pool to manage **bytes.Buffer** instances used for I/O operations, reducing the frequency of allocations.

Minimize Small Allocations

Small, frequent allocations can contribute disproportionately to GC overhead. Batching these allocations or using larger, pre-allocated slices can mitigate this issue.

Example of Batch Allocation:

Instead of allocating small slices in a loop, pre-allocate a larger slice and distribute portions as needed.

```go
largeSlice := make([]byte, 10000) // A large slice
smallSlices := make([][]byte, 100)
for i := range smallSlices {
    smallSlices[i] = largeSlice[i*100 : (i+1)*100] // Distributing portions of the large slice
}
```

Understand and Optimize Data Structures

Choosing the right data structure can have a significant impact on memory usage. For example, using maps with too many small objects as keys can increase memory usage due to the way Go implements maps. In such cases, consider alternatives that better suit your memory usage patterns.

Leverage **sync.Pool** for Frequently Used Complex Objects

For objects that are expensive to create and are used frequently, such as database connection objects or buffers for processing data, **sync.Pool** can be used to reuse these objects effectively.

Best Practices

- Profile your application to identify high memory usage areas. Go's pprof tool can help identify these spots.
- Be mindful of the lifecycle of your objects. Holding onto objects longer than necessary can prevent them from being garbage collected, leading to increased memory usage.
- Regularly review and optimize your data structures and algorithms to minimize memory allocations.

Recipe 4: Implementing Singleton for Database Connections

Scenario

In the context of establishing SQL database connectivity (as learned in a previous recipe), managing database connections efficiently is crucial for application performance and scalability. Creating multiple instances of the database connection can lead to resource leaks and performance issues. The Singleton design pattern ensures that only one instance of the database connection is created, providing a global point of access to it.

Singleton Pattern Implementation

The Singleton pattern restricts the instantiation of a class to one "single" instance and provides a global point of access to it. This is particularly useful for managing resources such as database connections.

Define a Singleton Structure for Database Connection

Create a struct that will hold the singleton instance of the database connection. Use **sync.Once** to ensure that the instance is only created once.

```
package main

import (

"database/sql"

"log"

"sync"

_ "github.com/lib/pq"
```

)

```go
type singletonDatabase struct {
    connection *sql.DB
}

var instance *singletonDatabase
var once sync.Once

func GetDatabaseInstance() *singletonDatabase {
    once.Do(func() {
        connStr := "user=username dbname=password sslmode=disable"
        db, err := sql.Open("postgres", connStr)
        if err != nil {
            log.Fatalf("Failed to open database: %v", err)
        }
        instance = &singletonDatabase{connection: db}
    })
    return instance
}
```

Using the Singleton Database Connection

Access the database connection through the **GetDatabaseInstance** method, which ensures that only one instance is ever created and used throughout the application.

```go
func main() {
```

    dbInstance := GetDatabaseInstance()

    // Use dbInstance.connection for database operations

}
```

*Benefits and Considerations*
- Controlled Access: The Singleton pattern provides controlled access to the database connection, ensuring that resource management is centralized.
- Lazy Initialization: The database connection is only created when it's needed, reducing startup time and resource usage.
- Thread-Safety: The use of **sync.Once** guarantees that the instance is created in a thread-safe manner, which is crucial in a concurrent environment like Go.

However, it's important to use the Singleton pattern judiciously, as it can introduce global state into an application, making testing more difficult and leading to tighter coupling between components.

# Recipe 5: Managing Dependencies and Go Modules Effectively

## Scenario

Think back on how far we've come in improving the library app, incorporating many packages for things like caching, database interactions, and more. Managing the program's dependencies becomes increasingly challenging as the application evolves. Maintaining application compatibility and security by checking that all packages are up-to-date is of the utmost importance. To make things easier, Go Modules provides a standardized and efficient method for dealing with dependencies.

## Practical Solution

### Initializing a New Module

If you haven't already, start by initializing a module in your project directory. This creates a **go.mod** file, which tracks your project's dependencies.

go mod init github.com/yourusername/yourprojectname
```

Adding Dependencies

When you import and use packages in your project, Go Modules will automatically add them to your **go.mod** file the first time you build your project or explicitly request to add or update dependencies.

For example, to add the Redis client and PostgreSQL driver used in previous recipes:

go get github.com/go-redis/redis/v8

go get github.com/lib/pq

These commands fetch the latest versions of these packages and update your **go.mod** and **go.sum** files, the latter of which tracks the expected cryptographic checksums of your dependencies.

Upgrading and Downgrading Dependencies

To upgrade or downgrade a specific dependency, use **go get** with the package and version number or use **go get -u** to update all dependencies to their latest minor or patch versions.

go get github.com/go-redis/redis/v8@v8.11.0

go get -u

Tidying Your Module

Over time, as dependencies are added, removed, or updated, your **go.mod** file might reference packages that are no longer needed. Use **go mod tidy** to remove these unused dependencies and ensure that your **go.mod** and **go.sum** files reflect the actual state of your module.

go mod tidy

Vendoring Dependencies

Although not always necessary with Go Modules, you might want to vendor your dependencies, especially for building offline or to ensure that you have a copy of all your dependencies within your project.

go mod vendor

Best Practices

- Regularly run **go mod tidy** to keep your module clean.
- Review changes in **go.mod** and **go.sum** files before committing them to version control to understand how your dependencies are evolving.
- Be cautious with major version updates of dependencies, as they may introduce breaking changes. Use semantic versioning to understand the nature of updates.

Summary

This chapter has all the information Go developers need to make their apps run faster, be easier to manage, and be more reliable. Beginning with tips for developing high-performance Go code, the chapter carefully explains how to use Go's concurrency model, memory management strategies, and the standard library to create efficient and fast applications. It emphasizes the significance of idiomatic Go techniques, such as avoiding excessive memory allocations and taking full advantage of Go's robust concurrency features to improve application performance and responsiveness.

The chapter progresses to profiling Go programs, where you'll learn about tools and strategies for identifying performance bottlenecks and optimizing code. It offers insight on effective memory management by disclosing ways for reducing garbage collection overhead and memory utilization, both of which are critical for high-performance applications. Furthermore, the investigation of design patterns and dependency management using Go Modules emphasizes the importance of structured coding practices and dependency hygiene in developing scalable, dependable, and readily maintainable software. You may successfully plan and manage large-scale Go applications by implementing design patterns such as Singleton for resource management and mastering Go Modules for project dependencies.

By the end of this chapter, you will have a comprehensive understanding of the complexities of optimizing Go programs not only for speed, but also for improved resource use, resulting in more scalable and resilient systems. The lessons in this chapter are crucial for you trying to push the frontiers of what you can achieve with Go, ensuring that your applications stand out in terms of performance, stability, and maintainability in today's software landscape.

Chapter 10: Networking and Protocol Handling

Introduction

Chapter 10, "Networking and Protocol Handling," takes a deep dive into Go's network programming, covering a broad range of protocols and techniques that are crucial for creating modern applications. This chapter teaches you how to build strong and efficient networked applications by understanding and implementing both common and complex networking protocols. You will learn how to handle a variety of networking tasks by following a number of practical recipes, from creating HTTP clients for web interactions to constructing FTP and SSH clients for file transfers and secure command execution.

Beginning with "Building Efficient HTTP Clients," the chapter covers the principles of developing and optimizing HTTP clients in Go, focusing on recommended practices for making requests, handling responses, and managing connections to achieve high performance in web communications. Moving on, "Implementing FTP and SSH Clients" investigates the development of clients for communicating with FTP servers for file operations and SSH servers for remote command execution, demonstrating Go's adaptability in network programming.

The research continues with "Designing and Implementing Custom Protocols," which walks you through the process of developing and implementing bespoke protocols tailored to specific application requirements, emphasizing Go's ability to handle complex networking logic. "Advanced WebSocket Programming" then delves into real-time, bidirectional communication between clients and servers, allowing the creation of interactive web applications.

Security is a top priority in network programming, therefore "Secure Communications with TLS/SSL" teaches you how to encrypt communication channels, protecting data integrity and secrecy during network interactions. Finally, "Constructing a Simple Web Server from Scratch" presents a step-by-step approach to developing a web server, combining the networking knowledge gained in previous chapters and applying it to properly deliver web content.

By the end of this chapter, you will have a full understanding of networking and protocol handling in Go, as well as the practical skills required to build sophisticated and secure networked applications. This knowledge foundation is invaluable in addressing the challenges of current network programming, ranging from simple data transmission to complicated, secure real-time communication systems.

Recipe 1: Building Efficient HTTP Clients

Scenario

Imagine developing a feature for the library application that requires fetching book metadata from an external RESTful API. This operation is frequent and critical for updating the catalog. Therefore, the HTTP client must be optimized for speed, efficient connection management, and error handling to ensure reliability and responsiveness.

Practical Solution

Use the *http.Client* with Custom Settings

The **http.Client** struct in Go allows customization of settings such as timeouts and connection pooling, which are crucial for efficiency.

```go
package main

import (
    "net"
    "net/http"
    "time"
)

func createHttpClient() *http.Client {
    netTransport := &http.Transport{
        Dial: (&net.Dialer{
            Timeout:   5 * time.Second,
            KeepAlive: 30 * time.Second,
        }).Dial,
        TLSHandshakeTimeout:   5 * time.Second,
        ExpectContinueTimeout: 1 * time.Second,
        MaxIdleConns:          100,
        IdleConnTimeout:       90 * time.Second,
    }
    httpClient := &http.Client{
```

```go
        Timeout: time.Second * 10,
        Transport: netTransport,
    }
    return httpClient
}
```

This client configuration includes a timeout for the entire request, including connection establishment, and customizes the transport to manage connections efficiently.

Making Concurrent Requests

When making multiple requests, for example, to fetch metadata for different books, utilize Go's concurrency model to make these requests in parallel, significantly reducing the overall latency.

```go
func fetchBookMetadata(client *http.Client, urls []string) {
    var wg sync.WaitGroup
    for _, url := range urls {
        wg.Add(1)
        go func(url string) {
            defer wg.Done()
            resp, err := client.Get(url)
            if err != nil {
                // handle error
                return
            }
            defer resp.Body.Close()
```

```go
    // Process response
}(url)
}
wg.Wait()
}
```

Best Practices
- Reuse the **http.Client** instance across requests to take advantage of connection pooling.
- Set appropriate timeouts to avoid hanging requests.
- Be mindful of server load and respect rate limits when making concurrent requests.

Recipe 2: Implementing FTP and SSH Clients

Scenario

Want to facilitate FTP and SSH clients in Go for the automation of file transfers and remote command execution, which can be essential for various administrative tasks, such as automated backups, system updates, or data synchronization processes.

Implementing an FTP Client

FTP (File Transfer Protocol) is widely used for transferring files between a client and a server over a network.

For FTP interactions, the **github.com/jlaffaye/ftp** package provides a convenient way to implement FTP client functionalities in Go.

```
go get github.com/jlaffaye/ftp
```

Example FTP Client for File Download

```go
package main

import (
```

```go
    "fmt"
    "github.com/jlaffaye/ftp"
    "io/ioutil"
    "log"
)

func main() {
    c, err := ftp.Dial("ftp.example.com:21", ftp.DialWithTimeout(5*time.Second))
    if err != nil {
        log.Fatal(err)
    }
    err = c.Login("user", "password")
    if err != nil {
        log.Fatal(err)
    }
    r, err := c.Retr("path/to/remote/file")
    if err != nil {
        log.Fatal(err)
    }
    defer r.Close()
    buf, err := ioutil.ReadAll(r)
    if err != nil {
```

```
log.Fatal(err)

}
```

fmt.Println("Downloaded file content:", string(buf))

```
if err := c.Quit(); err != nil {

log.Fatal(err)

}

}
```

Implementing an SSH Client

SSH (Secure Shell) is a protocol for operating network services securely over an unsecured network.

The **golang.org/x/crypto/ssh** package offers the tools needed to implement an SSH client in Go.

Example SSH Client for Running Remote Commands

```
package main

import (

"golang.org/x/crypto/ssh"

"log"

"os"

)

func main() {

config := &ssh.ClientConfig{

User: "user",

Auth: []ssh.AuthMethod{
```

```go
        ssh.Password("password"),
    },
    HostKeyCallback: ssh.InsecureIgnoreHostKey(),
}
conn, err := ssh.Dial("tcp", "example.com:22", config)
if err != nil {
    log.Fatal(err)
}
defer conn.Close()
session, err := conn.NewSession()
if err != nil {
    log.Fatal(err)
}
defer session.Close()
session.Stdout = os.Stdout
session.Stderr = os.Stderr
if err := session.Run("ls -lah"); err != nil {
    log.Fatal(err)
}
}
```

Best Practices

- Security: Always ensure secure handling of credentials and use secure connections. For SSH, prefer public key authentication over password authentication when possible.
- Error Handling: Implement comprehensive error handling and logging for network operations and authentication failures.
- Resource Management: Properly manage resources by closing connections, sessions, and readers/writers.

Recipe 3: Designing and Implementing Custom Protocols

Scenario

Imagine the library application needs a specialized communication protocol for a distributed cache system. This system should quickly synchronize cache updates across multiple instances. The standard protocols are either too heavy or not flexible enough for the specific data patterns and synchronization needs of the application. A custom lightweight protocol over TCP can be designed to meet these precise requirements.

Practical Solution

Define the Protocol

Start by defining the structure and rules of your custom protocol. For the cache synchronization use case, the protocol could specify message types such as **UPDATE**, **DELETE**, and **HEARTBEAT** to manage cache state and monitor the health of connections. Example message format:

[MESSAGE_TYPE][KEY_LENGTH][KEY][VALUE_LENGTH][VALUE]

Each segment of the message has a predefined length, except for the **KEY** and **VALUE**, which are variable and prefixed with their length.

Use Go's **net** package to establish TCP connections, through which the custom protocol messages will be sent and received.

Server Setup

Create a TCP server to listen for incoming protocol messages.

```
package main
```

```go
import (
    "bufio"
    "fmt"
    "net"
    "os"
)

func main() {
    listener, err := net.Listen("tcp", ":8080")
    if err != nil {
        fmt.Println(err)
        os.Exit(1)
    }
    defer listener.Close()
    for {
        conn, err := listener.Accept()
        if err != nil {
            fmt.Println(err)
            continue
        }
        go handleConnection(conn)
    }
```

}

```go
func handleConnection(conn net.Conn) {

scanner := bufio.NewScanner(conn)

for scanner.Scan() {

fmt.Println("Received message:", scanner.Text())

// Process message based on custom protocol

}

conn.Close()

}
```

Client Implementation

Implement a client that sends messages to the server following the custom protocol.

```go
package main

import (

"fmt"

"net"

)

func main() {

conn, err := net.Dial("tcp", "localhost:8080")

if err != nil {

fmt.Println(err)

return
```

}

defer conn.Close()

message := "UPDATE|3|key|4|data" // Simplified message format

conn.Write([]byte(message))

}

You can optimize efficiency and usefulness by designing and implementing a custom protocol in Go. This allows them to tailor communication mechanisms to their individual needs.... To address limitations of traditional protocols, you can take advantage of Go's networking features to build scalable, dependable, and efficient communication solutions. By allowing for granular control over the data exchange process, this method improves the capacity to operate distant systems, such as cache synchronization techniques.

Recipe 4: Standard WebSocket Programming in Go

Scenario

For example, imagine our library app is planning to implement real-time services like user-facing live chat or instantaneous book availability alerts. Because WebSockets eliminate the need for polling and enable the server to send messages to clients quickly, they are ideal for these functionalities.

Implementing a WebSocket Server in Go

Use the **gorilla/websocket** Package

The **gorilla/websocket** package is a popular Go library that provides robust support for working with WebSockets. It simplifies the process of upgrading HTTP connections to WebSocket connections.

go get github.com/gorilla/websocket

Create a Simple WebSocket Echo Server

This server will echo back any messages it receives from WebSocket clients.

```go
package main

import (

"fmt"

"log"

"net/http"

"github.com/gorilla/websocket"
)

var upgrader = websocket.Upgrader{

ReadBufferSize: 1024,

WriteBufferSize: 1024,

// Allow connections from any origin

CheckOrigin: func(r *http.Request) bool { return true },

}

func echoHandler(w http.ResponseWriter, r *http.Request) {

conn, err := upgrader.Upgrade(w, r, nil)

if err != nil {

log.Println(err)

return

}

defer conn.Close()
```

```go
for {
    messageType, message, err := conn.ReadMessage()
    if err != nil {
        log.Println(err)
        break
    }
    fmt.Printf("Received: %s\n", message)
    if err := conn.WriteMessage(messageType, message); err != nil {
        log.Println(err)
        break
    }
}
}
func main() {
    http.HandleFunc("/echo", echoHandler)
    log.Fatal(http.ListenAndServe(":8080", nil))
}
```

Implementing a WebSocket Client in Go

A simple client that connects to the WebSocket server and sends messages could be implemented as follows:

```go
package main
```

```go
import (
    "flag"
    "log"
    "os"
    "github.com/gorilla/websocket"
)
func main() {
    flag.Parse()
    log.SetFlags(0)
    url := "ws://localhost:8080/echo"
    c, _, err := websocket.DefaultDialer.Dial(url, nil)
    if err != nil {
        log.Fatal("dial:", err)
    }
    defer c.Close()
    // Sending a message to the server
    message := []byte("Hello, WebSocket!")
    if err := c.WriteMessage(websocket.TextMessage, message); err != nil {
        log.Println("write:", err)
        return
    }
```

```
// Reading the echo message from the server
_, message, err = c.ReadMessage()
if err != nil {
    log.Println("read:", err)
    return
}
log.Printf("Received: %s", message)
}
```

The gorilla/websocket package makes it easy for you to incorporate real-time capabilities into your applications by implementing WebSocket communication in Go. In order to build interactive and dynamic web apps, it is necessary to learn more advanced WebSocket programming. This includes things like handling numerous clients, broadcasting messages, and protecting WebSocket connections.

Recipe 5: Secure Communications with TLS/SSL

Scenario

Our library app is integrating real-time capabilities through WebSockets, therefore securing these connections is crucial for user data and privacy. Similarly, we should encrypt all traffic using HTTPS on any HTTP server we deploy. You will learn how to secure WebSocket connections with TLS and how to set up a basic HTTPS server in this recipe.

Implementing a TLS-secured HTTP Server

Generate TLS Certificates

For development purposes, you can generate a self-signed certificate using OpenSSL:

```
openssl req -x509 -nodes -days 365 -newkey rsa:2048 -keyout server.key -out server.crt
```

For production, consider obtaining certificates from a trusted CA like Let's Encrypt.

Create an HTTPS Server

Modify the HTTP server to serve content over HTTPS using the generated certificates.

```go
package main

import (
    "log"
    "net/http"
)

func handler(w http.ResponseWriter, r *http.Request) {
    w.Header().Set("Content-Type", "text/plain")
    w.Write([]byte("This is an example server.\n"))
}

func main() {
    http.HandleFunc("/", handler)
    log.Printf("Serving on https://0.0.0.0:8443")
    err := http.ListenAndServeTLS(":8443", "server.crt", "server.key", nil)
    if err != nil {
        log.Fatal(err)
    }
}
```

Securing WebSocket Connections with TLS

WebSocket connections, being initiated over HTTP, can be secured by simply securing the initial

HTTP connection. If your HTTP server is TLS-secured, any WebSocket upgrade from this server will inherently be secure (WSS).

Recipe 6: Constructing a Simple Web Server from Scratch

Scenario

For our library application, let us assume we want to develop a new feature that allows users to browse the catalog of books and reserve them through a web interface. This feature requires a web server to handle HTTP requests for serving the catalog data and processing reservation requests.

Practical Solution

Setting up the Server

Use the **http** package to set up a basic web server. The server will respond to two routes: one for fetching the book catalog and another for reserving a book.

```go
package main

import (
  "fmt"
  "log"
  "net/http"
)

func catalogHandler(w http.ResponseWriter, r *http.Request) {
  fmt.Fprintf(w, "This would return the book catalog.")
}

func reserveHandler(w http.ResponseWriter, r *http.Request) {
```

```go
// For simplicity, assume the book ID is passed as a query parameter

bookID := r.URL.Query().Get("bookID")

fmt.Fprintf(w, "This would reserve the book with ID: %s", bookID)

}

func main() {

http.HandleFunc("/catalog", catalogHandler)

http.HandleFunc("/reserve", reserveHandler)

fmt.Println("Starting server on :8080")

if err := http.ListenAndServe(":8080", nil); err != nil {

log.Fatal("ListenAndServe: ", err)

}

}
```

Running the Server

Execute the program. Your server is now running on **http://localhost:8080**. It listens for requests to **/catalog** and **/reserve**, responding with placeholder texts. In a real application, these handlers would interact with the backend to fetch data or perform actions based on the request.

Summary

Covering a wide range of techniques and protocols vital to contemporary web and network applications, this chapter led you through the complexities of Go network programming. Beginning with the development of efficient HTTP clients, the chapter progresses to the implementation of FTP and SSH clients, demonstrating Go's adaptability in handling a variety of network protocols and jobs. These early recipes provide a solid foundation, demonstrating how Go may be used to interface with many sorts of servers and services, supporting tasks ranging from file transfers to secure command execution via SSH.

As the chapter develops, it becomes more technical, covering subjects such as designing and implementing custom protocols, advanced WebSocket programming, secure communications with TLS/SSL, and building a web server from scratch. This trip prepares you to create custom communication solutions adapted to your application's demands, establish real-time data sharing with WebSockets, secure network connections, and build the backbone for web applications using Go's built-in HTTP server capabilities. The emphasis on security, particularly via TLS/SSL, emphasizes the significance of protecting data in transit, which is a vital feature of network programming in an era of extensive cybersecurity concerns.

Overall, this chapter improves your comprehension of network programming fundamentals while simultaneously demonstrating Go's rich capabilities and standard library support for developing scalable, secure, and efficient networked applications. By experimenting with various protocols and networking scenarios, you are better prepared to face the challenges of modern application development, ensuring that your projects can effectively communicate over the network, handle real-time interactions, and maintain high levels of security and performance.

Index

A

API development 66, 86, 87
Auth 191
Authentication 66, 74, 75, 124
Authorization 77

C

Caching 148, 165, 167, 171
Channels 26, 27
Command 109, 124, 126, 142
Cookie 115
CRUD operations 66, 72, 151, 154, 156, 161, 169
CSV processing 48

D

Database transactions 157

E

Error handling 2, 19

F

FTP client 188

G

Go Modules 4, 171, 181, 182, 183
Goroutines 26, 27

H

HTTP client 121, 185, 202
HTTP/2 90

K

Kafka 134

L

Logging 16, 89, 103, 104, 129, 138

M

Maps 9, 10
Message 81, 98
Microservices - 128, 129, 130, 132, 136, 138, 140, 143
Middleware 72, 73, 74, 77
Monitoring 89, 129, 138, 140

N

NATS 134
NoSQL database 159, 163, 169

P

Pointers 19, 20
Profiling 171, 174, 175, 176
Protocol 7, 90, 184, 185, 188, 192

R

REST API 30, 86
Routing 72

S

Session 109, 115, 116, 117
Singleton 179, 180, 181, 183
Singleton pattern 179, 181
Slices 9
SQL database 148, 154, 169, 179
SQL injection 154, 156
SSH client 185, 188, 190, 202
SSL certificates 101, 102
Strategy 167
Structs 9, 10, 19, 20

T

TLS/SSL ------------------------------- 107, 185, 199, 203

Token -- 77, 116

Epilogue

The trip we've taken together is now coming to an end as we turn the last pages. This path has been filled with discovery, challenges, and tremendous progress, from the early steps of setting up your Go environment to learning sophisticated topics like concurrency, networking, and performance optimization. My goal in writing this was to do more than simply provide you with instructions; I wanted to show you the ropes so that you could become an expert Go problem solver and think critically.

To provide a thorough grasp of Go's capabilities and best practices, we've handled a wide array of difficulties throughout this book, with each recipe designed to build on the preceding. With the information you've gained so far, you should be able to confidently navigate Go's environment and create apps that are efficient, resilient, and safe. Moreover, I wish that I have inspired in you an innate desire to know more and an enthusiasm for lifelong education, qualities that will serve you well in the dynamic field of software development.

New technologies appear, best practices change, and our abilities continuously increase—this is the joy of programming. If you want to learn Go, try new things, and make an impact in the community, the "Go Programming Cookbook" is a good place to start. Participate in online communities, help out open-source initiatives, and teach others what you know. Collaborating with people, exchanging ideas, and gaining knowledge from different viewpoints makes the learning process so much more fulfilling.

Going forward, Go programming has a very bright future. You should take the knowledge you gained from this book with you into the future, but you should also be receptive to fresh perspectives. Being flexible is essential for being up-to-date and creative in the software development industry, which is known for its rapid pace of change. Whether it's trying out new approaches to programming, working on innovative projects, or just thinking about different methods to solve problems, push yourself to think outside of your usual routine.

Finally, I want to say how much I appreciate being a part of your Go programming adventure. Your kindness is much appreciated. We genuinely want to see you succeed as a developer, and we wrote the "Go Programming Cookbook" with that goal in mind. Keep in mind that the difficulties you face along the way are really chances to learn more, grow as a person, and find what truly ignites your passions.

I appreciate you coming along on the ride. I wish you a future brimming with new ideas, breakthroughs, and achievements. Wishing you a future filled with more Go code, exciting projects that push you, and the opportunity to keep making a big splash in software development. Continue to code, continue to learn, and, above all, continue to enjoy the ride.

THANK YOU

Made in the USA
Las Vegas, NV
31 March 2024

88069735R00125